Sales Utopia

How to Get the Right People, Doing the Right Things, Enough Times.

By:
Mason Duchatschek and
Allen Minster

with contributions from Claudia Minster

Sales Utopia:
How to Get the Right People, Doing the Right Things, Enough Times.

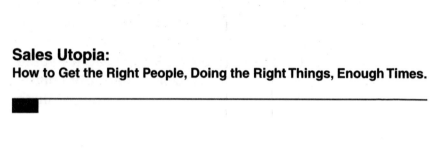

Copyright 1999 by Performance Press Worldwide, Inc.

Printed in U.S.A.

ISBN: 0-9674377-0-9
Library of Congress Catalog Card No. 99-90793

Dedication

This book is dedicated to God, through which all things are possible, and to the family members, clients, competitors, co-workers, teachers, coaches, and mentors who have helped us grow and develop. Thank you for your encouragement and support.

Contents

Introduction

If you're like us, you've probably had your fill of ivory tower opinions, egg-head concepts, and academic theories. It seems that anyone who ever worked as a salesperson or read a book on sales claims to be an expert on running a sales team. Like most fish tales, the longer it has been since they were in sales, the better they **were**. You know the type ...

In this book you'll find only field proven, real word strategies and tactics for taking your company to the next level. The people who wrote this book are in the field every day prospecting, solving customer problems, and closing business.

Our goal in writing this book was to introduce you to a whole new way of looking at the selection and sales process. In the companies we've worked with, we've found that there are processes for every aspect of the business day. There are processes for paying bills, managing accounts receivable, and manufacturing products, but when it comes to selection and selling, not only is there no process ... **everything is random**:

Selection of employees and sales staff is random

Training is random

Prospecting is random

Client contact is random

Cross selling is random

Referrals are random ...

... therefore, results are random!

Our intent in this book is to provide companies with information on processes that will increase sales and profitability.

This book is a collaborative effort from two company presidents who have worked together and with hundreds of entrepreneurs, senior executives, human resource managers, and top producing salespeople. Our clients include small firms, high growth companies, and Fortune 1000 corporations.

Mason Duchatschek is the president of AMO Employer Services, Inc. After working as a consultant for a nationally known sales and management consulting firm, he founded his own company in 1991. His initial goal was to provide employers with skill, attitude, and personality assessment tools that could help employers hire right the first time and identify training needs so current employees could perform at higher levels. Since then, tens of thousands of employees have been hired for, and are performing in, positions that best suit their abilities because of the technologies available through his company.

Allen and Claudia Minster are partners and co-founders of Performance Solutions, LLC., which specializes in delivering computer driven sales and marketing systems that are designed to turn information into sales. These systems have been installed in banks, stock brokerage firms, manufacturing companies, insurance agencies, and even non-profit corporations.

One final note. This book was intended to be a working document. It was written the way we talk to our clients, our prospects, and our employees. As you read the material please keep this in mind—**What we lack in "high gloss," we make up for in content!**

We wish you the best in all of your selling efforts.

Allen and Claudia Minster   Mason Duchatschek
Performance Solutions, LLC   AMO Employer Services, Inc.

Section 1:
A Commitment To Improvement

Like anyone, I've won some battles and lost others. Yet I've always sought to be an achiever. It has been my nature to put forth my best effort to prepare for and meet the challenges ahead. Victory lies in doing your best. If my best wasn't good enough, I sought out role models or coaches who could help. I sought to learn vicariously through the successes and short-comings of others without experiencing all the hassles that accompany a trial and error education.

I've always wanted to own my own business and was gifted with the entre-preneurial spirit at an early age. Kool-Aid stands went up in the neighbor-hood for the construction workers building homes in our subdivision. Work-ing at the swimming pool snack bar, I found it only logical to rent goggles for extra money. My first car was paid for before I reached the age of 16 and I paid for it by mowing lawns for real-estate companies, apartment com-plexes, and neighbors. During the summer, five to ten other kids mowed with and for me. The experience and responsibility of selling, managing, and supervising excited me.

Earning a college degree in business didn't create a delusion that "book smarts" would make me ready to take on the world. I wasn't masochistic by nature so the idea of "hard knocks" wasn't particularly appealing either. Of course, "hard knocks" are part of the growth process. Fortunately, unnecessary hardships can be avoided when you have good coaches. I searched for coaches in books and seminars. Common sense told me to find experts who had succeeded in the business arena. Modeling their strategies could only help to shorten my learning curve, minimize my tribulations, and allow me to achieve greater results faster.

I selected "real world" coaches and models carefully. In a practical sense, it was tough to be enamored with the mumbo jumbo theories and philosophies of academics who had never competed in the business arena. It was much easier for me to be impressed by those entrepreneurs who combined the fundamentals learned in academia with their own sweat and common sense to become successful.

I attended Westminster College, a small, private, liberal-arts college in Fulton, Missouri. Fortunately for me, the business school faculty realized the need to expose students to more than textbooks. Frequently, successful alumni would return to campus to share their insights and describe real-life applications of our newfound knowledge. This small college had the vision to blend academics with the experiences of enthusiastic and supportive alumni, thereby enhancing the whole experience.

One year after college, my professional career began when I accepted a sales position working for a nationally known sales trainer and motivational speaker. He was unbelievably talented and had a tremendous work ethic. He made it possible for me to travel around the country promoting his sales training seminars to automotive dealerships. It was an outstanding opportunity for me to develop personally and professionally. At age twenty-two I was lucky to find a unique and wonderful opportunity to meet and work with world class authorities on selling, leadership, and management. Listening to educational tapes and reading books filled almost every spare moment. In the field, when and where it counted, opportunities presented themselves to apply the strategies and techniques I learned from the books and tapes.

My results kept pace with my ever increasing knowledge. Earnings during my first month in a sales territory were nearly $7000 in commissions. Back then, that wasn't bad income for someone only twenty-two years old!

I paid attention to what clients and prospects were telling me. After watching companies spend tens of thousands of dollars on training, it hit me. Why would clients and other successful companies spend so much money on training and yet ignore the causes of the problems that held them back? Worse yet, why would the very companies that needed help stubbornly resist the need to educate, train, and continually develop their most valuable asset ... their employees? Why would employees, working for companies with excellent training and educational opportunities, not take full advantage of what was available?

Could it be that current employees weren't a good fit for the demands of their jobs? Could it be that the companies were hiring new people who weren't a good fit for the jobs either?

On more than one occasion, shortsighted executives have complained that training is expensive. They feared they wouldn't recover the investment they made in training if the participating employees left the company prematurely. Paul D. Cummings once told me, "If you think education is expensive, consider the cost of ignorance!" Worse yet, they feared that their newly trained employee would leave and go to work for a competitor. The thought that they could be training their future competitors was repulsive. Perhaps they should have considered the alternative; having untrained, uneducated, unmotivated, and dissatisfied salespeople staying.

I thought to myself again and again, "If only there were a way to help frustrated sales managers and business owners get the right people in the right positions!" The right work force would quickly develop all the business opportunities one could ever want!" Clearly, there was an itch in the marketplace. I just had to figure out how to help companies scratch it.

I set out to discover the tools and strategies available to help business owners and sales managers hire the right employees the first time. I spent several years researching selection methods for salespeople. In fact, about that time, Michigan State University's School of Business did a study on hiring methods and their ability to predict success in the workplace. (More detail on that study is available in the book, *Building a Winning Team* by Harris Plotkin.) The study showed that pre-employment psychological or personality testing was the single most effective means of predicting the future success of job applicants. By comparison, information gained from testing was several times more reliable than information gained in interviews, examinations of experience, or evaluations based on the education of the applicants.

After analyzing hundreds of skill, attitude, and personality based assessment tools, I bought the rights and licenses to market what I found to be the most accurate and cost effective instruments available. I launched my own company in the early 90s to provide clients with access to the information they needed to hire more effective people and to get more results from their current staff. I wanted to make sure that these tools could be easily administered, quickly scored, and easily analyzed by any sales executive or business owner. I also wanted to make sure the tools were accurate and in compliance with guidelines established by the Equal Employment Opportunity Commission (EEOC) and the American's with Disabilities Act (ADA), along with federal, state, and local regulations.

As my familiarity with the information available through these assessments increased, so did my awareness of the different uses for this information. I realized that companies could utilize this type of data to analyze the strengths and weaknesses of their current sales force. Companies could use this data to identify and target training and developmental needs at both the individual and group levels.

I expected a grateful world to beat down my door, to thank me for providing a much needed service. I found out the hard way that it wasn't enough to identify a glaring need in the marketplace or a cost effective and easy to implement solution. I found out that I needed an efficient way to get our message to the prospects desirous of buying what I was selling. I was referred by a client to Allen Minster, who was featured on the cover of <u>Selling</u> magazine and consistently written about in numerous other publications. After meeting Allen, my company purchased his automated system, and implemented his strategies. Our growth from that point on was exponential.

Hundreds of major corporations are now clients of ours because of those strategies and the technology designed to implement them. I look forward to sharing the best of those strategies with you. This information will be an eye-opener and a welcome dose of common sense to even the most seasoned and knowledgeable sales executives and company presidents.

I assure you, I'm not talking about purely academic ideas. I'm talking about field tested strategies with proven results that let you cut right through what gets in your way and get the most for your sales and marketing dollar!

One of the most exciting things about my field is that on a daily basis I have the privilege of working with company presidents and senior sales executives of Fortune 500 companies as well as emerging and growing companies. Clients and prospective clients have proven to be a tremendous source of practical knowledge. You learn things across the desk from successful executives that you simply can't get anywhere else.

My clients and prospective clients share their greatest challenges with me.

They share their strategies and tactics. They let me know what's working and what isn't. I've listened to them carefully and learned both leading edge concepts and practical knowledge—not from people who *talk* about business, but from people who *do* business. What I learn from one client or prospective client enhances my ability to offer value to other businesses in similar situations. I'm going to share some of the best information I've learned with you.

Our purpose is to eliminate the junk getting in the way of your sales team's ability to achieve its potential! We want you to be aware of common sense strategies and tools that can help you make a difference, without turning everything upside down and creating chaos. It's a simple three-step process. First, focus on what's most important. Second, focus on continuous improvement. Third, keep doing it.

What's most important? Make sure you have the right people, doing the right things, enough times. That's it. Getting the right people in the right positions is an employee selection issue. Making sure they're doing the right things is an employee assessment and development issue. Ensuring they're making enough sales calls is a productivity issue best addressed whenever possible through automated systems.

I'm not saying that the little things aren't important. They are, but only **after** what's **most important** is taken care of first. After the fundamentals and basics are in place, then work on every little advantage you can get. They add up.

Friend or Foe?

I don't know of a tactful way to say this, but if I don't say it, no one else will. What I'm about to say can make all the difference in whether or not the strategies in this book can help you.

Before we begin, you need to make sure that you're not getting in the way of your sales team's ability to achieve their potential. Too many owners and sales executives achieve a limited degree of success that makes them too comfortable. When overconfidence and complacency set in, it's the beginning of the end. Your attitudes, good or bad, will permeate your entire working environment. Don't expect others to commit to excellence if you won't. Don't expect others to look for better ways if you don't.

The hero and the hypocrite both can tell you what needs to be done. One generates enthusiasm, esprit de corps, and support. The other generates resentment. Attitude is the variable that separates those with otherwise equal abilities.

How well is your sales team really doing? Compared to what? This is an important point. In my opinion there are too many executives coasting on "autopilot," falsely convinced that they are doing a great job simply because they are doing better than their competitors. Bad assumption!

If you are beating your competitors, great! Don't relax! Don't coast! You and your sales team ought to be comparing yourselves to what you're capable of doing! You should be your own toughest competitor! Beating your best should be the expectation, the standard! Not sometimes ... all the time!

Let me tell you about Roger Stork, the Director of Sales for Purina Mills, the nation's leader in the animal nutrition industry. If you were to define the criteria for a sales force that leads its field, it's Purina Mills. When I first met him, it didn't take long to recognize their absolute command of their market. He had over 400 salespeople nationwide, dominating their competition and had only around 10% turnover. That's quite impressive when you consider that many good companies experience two to three times that rate of turnover. Some companies have as much as five to ten times that rate of turnover.

When he learned that we existed to help companies improve their sales performance, he didn't say anything about how satisfied or comfortable he was with how things were going, (when by almost anyone else's standards he could have.) "I believe we can do better" is what he told me. He wanted more information, ways to use it, more convenient and faster ways to access that information so he could more effectively select and develop his sales team.

What kind of example does he set? Do you think his reps are "satisfied" or "comfortable" with their performance? Or do you think they want to know what else they can do?

Your salespeople should be doing their best and continually striving to make their best better through the acquisition of new skills and knowledge. *You* must set that expectation. We'll tell you how!

Section 2:
Hire Right... The First Time!

"Hire and hope." Does that define your strategy for selecting salespeople? If so, you'd better reevaluate. Quickly. How capable is a fish out of water or Tarzan out of the jungle? Why try forcing a square peg into a round hole? You owe it to yourself, your company, and the person being considered, to do all within your power to make sure the person you have, or are considering for a sales position, is a good fit for the demands of that job.

My experience has been that most sales driven companies do a very poor job of filling sales positions with people who are truly a good fit for the demands of the job. There are several reasons for this. Some sales executives don't understand the importance of doing it right the first time and rely on ineffective methods because—you've heard the phrase a thousand times—"That's the way we've always done it." Still others are convinced that they can make a successful salesperson out of anyone. Maybe they can, but at what cost in terms of time and money? Doesn't it only make sense to hire people who already have the "raw materials" necessary?

I believe the old cliché that "an ounce of prevention is worth a pound of cure." My mother used to tell me, "If you don't have the time to do something right the first time, you certainly won't have the time to do it over."

Quality management "gurus" say that for every dollar invested in making sure things are done right the first time, a company can expect to save ten to twenty times that amount in correcting a problem on the back end.

There is more to consider than just recruiting and training costs. Sure, it costs money to place advertisements, pay managers for their interviewing and decision making time, and absorb applicable travel and relocation expenses. But those dollars are only the beginning. Using headhunters escalates costs still further. Often overlooked is the cost of lost sales and missed opportunities in an uncovered or ineffectively covered sales territory during transitional periods between old and new salespeople.

In the life insurance industry, general agents will tell you that the cost to get one agent recruited and trained well enough to make it in their industry is well over $200,000. Here's another way of looking at the importance of hiring right. Calculate the difference between the annual sales production of your best and worst representative. Over the course of ten years, to what sum will that difference amount in lost profit to your company? Can you afford not to hire the best sales representatives available?

What will be the impact on your customers from turnover caused by hiring the wrong people? Do you really know? If you expect repeat sales, you will have to provide ongoing service. You will have to make possible the close business relationships that only a long term sales representative can provide. The magnitude of a single hiring mistake can be devastating.

In the political arena, botched diplomatic relations can mean little or no trade with a country for very long periods of time. We have numerous clients in the wholesale food industry, where salespeople sell and service orders for food from restaurants, schools and nursing homes, etc. The consensus among our clients is that trust and good working relationships take time to build. Just as in politics, one bad representative can destroy in a relatively short period of time much of what those before him had worked long and hard to accomplish.

If the average salesperson gets paid $40,000 per year and stays 10 years, you are about to invest nearly half a million dollars in an effort to gain market share. If you were going to invest a half a million dollars in a piece of machinery or equipment, would you simply trust the feeling in your gut? Given the choice, wouldn't you test it, analyze it and amass as much valuable information as you could before making a decision?

Here's another question. If you were going to invest half a million dollars in a piece of equipment, would you choose an employee who knew little or nothing about how the equipment was supposed to be used to evaluate its merit? Be careful how you answer this one! If I called your company and told you that I could help you hire better salespeople, to whom would you tell me to talk?

If you think human resources is the answer, you're just like eight out of ten other companies. And if that's what you think, you can kiss your opportunity for a competitive advantage good-bye! Think again! Human resource professionals do important work. They find themselves in the center of things and never get the credit and respect they deserve for the important work they do. That's the problem! Most of them feel like they are unappreciated, and rightfully so.

However, when it comes to additional tasks like evaluating and scoring assessment technologies for salespeople, many of them balk at the idea; not because it's not a good idea, but because their personal agenda takes precedence over the company's needs. Don't blame them. It's not their fault. Most of you in their situation would do the same thing. Would you welcome additional work and responsibilities if you knew you wouldn't get paid any more and someone else would get to take the credit for the job you were doing?

In addition, I'm amazed at how many companies expect human resource personnel; people who in most cases have never been involved in sales, people who don't often like or even understand sales, to take on such a major responsibility. (In fairness, there are notable exceptions to this rule. Dedicated and progressive human resource professionals do exist who can do an outstanding job of teaming with the sales department to get results. But that's not the norm.)

As a corporate president, you're responsible for the bottom line. Half of the gross profit formula is sales revenue. Who cares more about that than you? Sure, you're busy and important, but so are revenues! Delegate something else! Get involved in this!

As a sales executive or manager, your credibility is on the line every day. You have to make your forecasts, or the boss will get someone else who can. You were probably a great salesperson, but now your job security and income is tied to the sales performance of others! With all that's at stake, don't you think you would want to know whether that new hire is going to be a superstar or a mistake? (If you don't, rest assured that your replacement will!)

How's it Going?

If hiring right is so important to your success, how well is your current hiring system working?

I can remember a client telling me that his current hiring methods helped him hire some great salespeople. The problem he found was that using the exact same methods, he had also hired other salespeople he wished he hadn't. Can you relate?

Why continue to rely on methods that have only proven they can't help you predict, with any reasonable degree of certainty, the likelihood that someone will succeed in sales?

What are you looking for? What should you be looking for? How do you know if you're getting it?

One of my favorite authors is a sales-trainer on the east coast named Bill Brooks. In a conversation we had on the phone one day, he told me that in his opinion the key to identifying the criteria most critical for job success, or the dimensions that typically separate those who are a good fit for a job from those who aren't, are their skills, attitudes, values, and behaviors.

Bill went on to describe how skills such as closing, handling objections, prospecting, time management, telephone technique, and presentation ability among other skills, let you know if a person CAN sell.

Dr. Greg Lousig-Nont, an internationally acclaimed hiring expert and developer of an outstanding sales skill assessment called the Sales Success Profile which measures thirteen critical sales skills, asks clients, " Would you prefer that your doctor had the skills of a doctor or the personality of a doctor?" He makes a good point. If you're going to send a rep into the field, shouldn't that rep know how to sell?

A poor set of sales skills doesn't mean you should eliminate an applicant from consideration. You just need to be prepared to spend extra time and resources to teach him or her how to sell effectively.

An example? In the retail wine industry, the majority of annual sales take place between the months of October and January. If a sales manager has to hire a new sales rep in the middle of September (assuming that all else is equal between two applicants), the wiser move is to lean toward the more skilled salesperson. In March, the pressure might not be as great to hire someone with sales skills.

Attitudes reflect whether or not prospective sales reps WILL sell. Do they have a work ethic? Are they call reluctant? Are they afraid to prospect? To speak in public? To ask for referrals? To cold call? Are they embarrassed to call themselves salespeople, etc? When would you want to know ... before or after you invest your time and resources?

Values reflect WHY people sell. If the job doesn't give them what is most important to them, they'll be unhappy and leave ... or worse ... be unhappy and stay! For example, if the job pay is based a hundred percent on commission and it's more important to the applicant to have a predictable pay scale and security, you will want to know that before you make an offer. If the applicant is more introverted and values solitude more than mixing with clients and prospects, how much do you think that individual will like outside sales?

Behavior reflects HOW people sell. Are they organized, or not organized at all? Are they too rigid or too flexible? Are they competitive? Do they have a sense of urgency and hustle? Are they completely insensitive or too sensitive? Are they too assertive? Too submissive?

Behavior is a very important dimension to explore. Training can mask behavioral tendencies to a degree, but under tremendous stress or pressure people tend to revert to their most natural and ingrained tendencies. Your job is to identify those tendencies and to decide to what degree they enhance or inhibit an applicant's ability to excel on the job.

I can recall a client who insisted that his company had the means to measure all but sales skills through traditional employee selection practices (i.e. interviewing, resumes, references, etc.). He chose only to use our sales skills assessment and relied on "their way" to evaluate applicant's attitudes, values, and behavioral style. Unfortunately, but not surprisingly, an applicant did very well on the sales skill assessment—and all "their methods"—yet failed miserably.

Clearly, the applicant knew how to sell. Further investigations, through testing, indicated that among other things, the individual drastically lacked the behavioral trait of assertiveness. In a textbook context, the person knew what to do, but didn't feel comfortable enough to do it!

Salespeople can react the same way a cat does to water if a given job doesn't closely fit their natural behavioral tendencies. If you walk to the end of a dock and throw a cat into the water, you'll find that cats have the skill to swim. They don't like to do it, but they can swim to shore. You can throw them in the water again, again, and again—and the results will be the same. But you can't expect a cat to wake up one morning and decide to go for a swim on its own. Additional "swimming lessons" and "training" won't enhance the cat's desire to get in the water. It doesn't come naturally to them.

Reference checks ... What job applicant is going to ask you to call someone who will tell you anything negative? Don't expect to get any really meaningful data from this source. Every once in awhile you may get a glimmer of insight or a warning, but don't expect too much.

Recently, I spoke with one company's vice president of sales who was complaining that he had just fired a sales rep for stealing. He had hired the sales rep from a competitor. He felt that he couldn't call them as a reference for the obvious reason that he assumed the applicant was still working for the competitor. As it turned out, the applicant hadn't worked for the previous employer for four months and just pretended to give two-weeks notice. He had in fact been fired for stealing.

He reported the incident to the police only to have them tell him that since no one was killed and no drugs were involved, they weren't going to press charges. The former employee, now fired twice for stealing from two different companies, was free to go and take advantage of some other unwitting organization.

In case you're curious, the thief who was just fired again for stealing had the audacity to list his most recent employer as a reference!   For fear of being sued, the vice president of sales who shared this story with me will only agree to verify employment dates to anyone who calls him.

As you might imagine, background verifications can be very helpful. If you feel that it is necessary to do a criminal records check, experience has taught me not to have a false sense of security if a record comes back clean. As the vice president of sales I just mentioned found out the hard way, the possibility exists that the applicant still participated in activities that may have been inappropriate. Maybe the culprit just wasn't caught. Maybe he was caught but there wasn't enough evidence to stand up in court. Maybe no one wanted to press charges.

It's surprising how many people claim to have educational degrees and work experience they don't have. Fortunately, it's not too difficult to identify gaps in employment, lack of credentials, or motor vehicle and criminal records that applicants would prefer you not know about. If they don't hesitate to misrepresent themselves to you, why would you expect them to treat your customers any differently?

When buying a pre-owned automobile, don't you ask about any previous wrecks or damage not immediately visible? Why wouldn't you want to know about blemishes on an applicant's record when knowing would minimize your risk? New hires don't come with warranties, and you can't exchange them. When it comes to employment, you have a right to know what you're getting, but you have to ask and to look for it!

Failure to investigate backgrounds can not only limit your ability to make an informed hiring decision, but can also create significant and unnecessary liabilities. For example, if you were to give a company car to a salesperson with no driving license or a string of DWI's, you are inviting a lawsuit. Under the concept of "Negligent Hiring" your company will be liable for damages caused, and it is your responsibility to your other employees, customers and your community to ensure that this salesperson is not a risk or likely to cause harm.

It's not hard, time consuming or expensive, to conduct these types of searches. Companies like ours can actually provide you with software that allows you to do this type of screening confidentially and conveniently using your own personal computer.

Resumes and applications are more of an exercise in creative writing than a record of facts, but you have to start somewhere. One of my clients put it best when they told me a resumé was like a "balance sheet with no liabilities."

A good friend and mentor of mine, Syd Robinson, once joked that, "Resumes should be listed in the library under fiction!"

Experts generally agree that approximately one third of all resumes are embellished. Some experts estimate as much as seventy percent of all applications contain some degree of false information. The problem becomes self-evident. For the sake of discussion, let's presume that half of the information you have on an applicant is accurate. Which half is accurate? Which half is falsified? How can you expect to make informed hiring decisions based on faulty premises?

Interviews are very popular as an employee selection method since you get a quality opportunity to observe an applicant's ability to communicate both orally and non-verbally.

Mary Rudder, a well known industrial/organizational psychologist best known for her expertise in helping companies design interviewing systems, told me that in her opinion most interviews lack bite for several reasons. "Most interviewers don't know what to ask. They don't know how to effectively evaluate the responses and they aren't prepared."

Often the applicants know the questions better than the interviewer. There are an abundance of resources to help applicants beat the interviewer. Go check out your local library or bookstore. You will see rows of books on how to interview. Some applicants actually hire career coaches and get videotapes of themselves doing "mock" interviews.

The lack of quantity and quality information about an applicant in a typical hiring process puts the interviewer at a decided disadvantage. We've talked about the deficiencies of the most popular methods; however, as Frank Kellert, a human resources consultant from Oklahoma City told me, "When assessing the candidacy of an applicant for a sales position, the least useful data I receive are the words that come from a call-reluctant person's mouth."

Trial periods were, according to the Michigan State University study I mentioned earlier, the second most effective method of predicting success in the workplace. David D'Arcangelo, a very popular author and speaker once said that, "If pilots learned to fly by trial and error, we would all be dead." So even the second most effective method leaves room for improvement.

Pre-employment skill, attitude and personality based assessments are, in my opinion, the most efficient and cost-effective method of gathering accurate and useful data. Good assessments can indicate the degree to which candidates given to misrepresentation are trying to exaggerate or make themselves appear more desirable. Assuming you have defined the type of person who excels in your sales organization (an assumption we will discuss in more detail later), it can be a simple task to identify how closely a person matches that model.

Some ill-informed, but well-meaning executives stay away from testing because they think they could get sued. News Flash ... companies can get sued for anything. Not utilizing what is arguably the best method to select quality employees with all that's at stake is nuts! Following the same logic, you should stop all advertising to avoid being sued for libel or false advertising! Heck, you shouldn't even open your doors. A customer could trip, fall, hurt himself and sue!

Professionally designed assessments must undergo rigorous validation studies to prove that they accurately and consistently measure what they are designed to without discriminating against any protected class (i.e.: age, race or sex, etc.). As with anything else, there are simple guidelines to follow, but by staying within those guidelines you should be able to avoid any problems.

I happen to prefer paper and pencil assessments scored and interpreted by a computer. A program that generates reports based on applicants' responses eliminates many potential biases. It doesn't care whether a person is black, white, blue, male, female, or Martian!

You can score the assessments on-site at your company and get immediate feedback. You can utilize the data to help you decide if the candidate will go to the next step in the hiring process. You can take the data from your reports and do targeted and meaningful interviews. You can compare applicants to models pre-established from analyzing groups of your top performers.

You know that old saying, "United we stand, divided we fall?" The same can be said for relying too heavily on information gathered from one employee selection method. I believe that the greatest success in hiring comes from a diligent, meticulous, and consistent selection process utilizing all of the above methods in conjunction with a well-organized pre-employment testing program to ensure a job match. The more information you have, the less likely you are to be surprised. Quantity and quality information is what you're after. Get it. Use it.

A study by Herbert M. Greenberg and Jeanne Greenberg called "Job Matching for Better Sales Performance" was written up in the October 1980 edition of the Harvard Business Review. The study indicated that in an industry with traditionally high turnover, when a job match was used to hire salespeople, less than one out of four new salespeople hired either quit or were fired in the first six months. The number of new salespeople hired who either quit or were fired in the first six months was nearly twice as high when a job match wasn't used!

In a similar study in an industry typically characterized by low turnover, the differences were even more dramatic. When a job match was used, approximately five percent quit or were fired in the first six months. Turnover was five times higher in the same period of time when a job match wasn't used.

Section 3:
Doing The Right Things... Assessment

Assessment Strategies

"If a person is not performing as expected, it is probably because they are miscast for the job."

- W. Edwards Deming

A doctor who operates without taking the time to do an analysis is heading for malpractice. How much confidence would you have in a doctor who tried to send you into the operating room to have a leg amputated when all you had was a sprained wrist? Sales reps act the same way when managers don't really understand what's going on. That's why it's important for you to take the time to find out.

Stage 1: Identify What You Need

What does it take for a salesperson to be his or her best in your company?

What skills, attitudes, behaviors, and values should be in place?

Consider the following skills:

*Dr. Greg Lousig-Nont did an extensive national study to identify the skills most commonly sought after by sales managers. "There was a consensus on thirteen areas that are as follows: (1) "Approaching and involving" a customer in the buying process in such a way that the salesman builds immediate rapport without alienating the prospect. (2) "Handling and answering objections" from potential clients. (3) "Closing" or asking for the sale. (4) Being able to strike a balance between being aggressive enough to ask for the sale and sensitive enough to know when they might be turning off the prospect. (5) "Honesty" in dealing with current and prospective clients. (6) Asking questions that helped identify needs and motivations for making a purchase. (7) Handling customer problems and problem customers with a willingness to listen, to understand, and to pursue satisfactory solutions. (8) "Qualifying" prospective clients. (9) "Prospecting and cold calling" effectively and efficiently. (10) Giving productive demonstrations and presentations. (11) "Managing time" in such a way to maximize profit potential. (12) Using the telephone effectively to generate interest in their product and arrange appointments. (13) Being enthusiastic about getting out and making sales contacts."

I would add that basic skills are valuable as well. A salesperson could be held back by a limited vocabulary or poor grammar, by deficiencies in basic math or spelling.

Consider the following attitudes:

Basic attitudes should include a positive work ethic and a sense of reliability! You should also know that there is a whole field of psychology that studies the attitudes and science of call reluctance. The leaders in that field, George W. Dudley and Shannon Goodson, authored an entire book

*Reprinted with permission, G.M. Lousig-Nont, Ph.D. copyright 1999

called, *"Earning What You're Worth? The Psychology Of Sales Call Reluctance"* and developed an assessment called the *"SPQ-Gold"* which is designed to identify call reluctance in current or prospective sales representatives.

If you take the time to read their book, you will realize the importance of this highly specialized science. You will find yourself asking new questions about your current and prospective sales representatives: Are they ashamed to tell people they're in sales? Or are they proud of their profession? Are they afraid to call on friends, relatives, or people they think have achieved a greater social status in our society? Do they think that prospecting is "tacky" or "beneath them"? Are they afraid of using the telephone to prospect for appointments? Do they fear being unprepared and avoid making sales contacts? Are they afraid to speak in front of groups? If so, what can be done about it?

Consider the following behaviors:

How do your representatives respond to challenges? Are they assertive or submissive? Do they tend to take charge or wait to be taken charge of? How do they attempt to influence and relate to others? Are they outgoing, "bubbly" and emotional or are they much more factual, logical, and low-keyed? Are they overly sensitive to the needs of others or are they insensitive? How trusting are they of others? Are they cynical or an easy mark? Are they competitive?

What is the pace at which they work? Do they prefer to work at a steady and deliberate pace in a predictable, unchanging work environment? Or do they like the thrill of numerous challenges and constant change? How do they respond to rules and regulations? Are they flexible or rigid?

What types of behavioral traits are of value? Neal Johnston, president of Advanced Psychometrics, Inc., in San Antonio, Texas and developer of many well-known pre-employment assessments, once told me that he founded his company because he felt that many assessments on the market measured behavioral areas of marginal value in the business environment. In his opinion, some of the most important and relevant behavioral traits include: Organization, sensitivity, imagination, flexibility, tension, probing level, assertiveness, and competitiveness.

Consider the following values:

Does the job give your salespeople what's most important to them? Does the job require your reps to go against any of their core beliefs?

Can you imagine a salesperson willing to sell tobacco products if a family member had died from a tobacco related illness? Could you imagine a salesperson actively promoting alcohol if his or her childhood was marred by alcoholic parents? Do your reps place a high value on being close to their family and object to frequent travel? Do they place a high value on acquiring knowledge and growing professionally, finding themselves bored with stagnant job duties?

Consider the value a person places on the different types of recognition. Some salespeople prefer a salary and are paralyzed by the fear of working one hundred percent on commission because they value security. Others place more value on the freedom to earn what they feel they are worth.

Some reps have a very high need to socialize and want to be around other people. In extreme cases, some reps can place such a high value on social relationships that they are more interested in making friends with the people they call on than they are in gaining customers. When working with existing clients, they stop asking for additional business because they fear causing harm to the relationship. On the other end of the spectrum, sales reps who have an extraordinarily low need to socialize probably prefer not to be around so many people and might find higher job satisfaction doing something else!

What you should want to know is the ideal degree to which salespeople should exhibit these traits to fit the ideal demands of a sales job in your company. You should also want to know where your salespeople deviate from the ideal range on each of these traits. Knowing that, you can take corrective action.

Stage 2: Assess Everyone-Identify What You Have

Where do you start? Frank Sproule, another mentor and successful corporate performance consultant, has been known to ask clients, "If you don't know what made you a great team, how can you expect to continue the process?"

Frank once asked me, "Have you ever been mismanaged? What was your productivity like while you were being mismanaged? Did the person who mismanaged you ever try to fix things?"

He explained further, "If you were investing tens of thousands of dollars a year on computer systems and software, would you expect an operator's manual to tell you what buttons to push to get the results you wanted? Of course you would, particularly if the system was networked and you needed multiple systems communicating and working together to get the best results. Unfortunately, sales reps don't come with operator's manuals and they are arguably much more important than any computer hardware or software programs."

Take inventory of your "human assets." There are numerous tools and technologies available to help you make this a quick and easy process.

Computer scored skill, attitude, behavior, and values assessments are available. They are cost-effective and can accurately measure the presence, absence, and intensity of what's most important to a person's ability to get the job done. The information can be used as an "operator's manual" for your salespeople to identify individual developmental needs, and can serve as a model to hire against in the future.

Assess your entire sales force! Learn what it is that makes your top per-formers top performers. Learn why people not doing well aren't doing well. Learn what it's going to take to get those in the middle of the pack to per-form at a level closer to that of your top performers!

Stage 3: Build Models Of Your Top Performers

Use the computerized assessment scoring software to build "success pat-terns" made from the analysis of the skill, attitude, behavior, and value ranges of your best salespeople. Eliminate the guesswork. Evaluations of salespeople based entirely on managers' opinions are about as reliable as measurements taken with a ruler made of rubber.

Once you have the pattern to use as a benchmark, analyze differences between individual reps and the success patterns and models of the top performers. Gaps will identify your specific developmental needs.

Stage 4: Take Appropriate Action.

Now that you know where your representatives need help, give it to them. (We'll discuss personal developmental options a little later.) You can clearly see what it will take to get your sales reps from where they are to where they need to be.

In some cases, the time, energy, and resources necessary to boost the performance of someone who is truly a "misfit" for the job may be prohibi-tive. If you have people who are doing just enough to keep from getting fired, but will never be top producers, they're wasting a territory that could be getting put to much better use.

Once you identify average or under-achievers who are clearly misfits given the demands of the job, you have the option of finding other positions in your company where they may be more of an asset than a liability. Consider encouraging them to make a "lateral move." On the other hand, you may prefer to encourage them to seek employment opportunities elsewhere. Chances are they don't like what they are doing anyway and just need a little encouragement to leave.

Once you identify the "misfits," you can plan to staff accordingly without any surprises. When it comes time to replace the "misfits," use the success pattern or model of the top performers as a benchmark for the pre-employment assessment of future job applicants. Make sure the new hires are better for their work than the ones you're getting rid of.

Warning!!!!!!!!!! The possibility exists that you may have a few under-achievers who match your success pattern. Chances are you may have even considered firing them. Don't do it yet. Look deeper, something else is affecting their performance. Maybe they happen to be in the same territory as your competitor's number one salesperson. Maybe the demographics of the territory aren't right for your product or service. Consider switching these employees into another territory or putting them on a new sales team. The possibility exists that there is a conflict with the manager or other team members. Maybe there are problems at home that need to be addressed because they are affecting work performance. Maybe they aren't making enough sales calls—and if that's the case, we'll talk about how to handle that situation in the later chapters of the book.

---

*Bonus Assessment/Development Strategy:

You may wish to consider a deeper assessment such as a 360-degree assessment with current salespeople who are a quality fit with the demands of the job. It's worth the investment since you know the people you would have participate have what it takes to do the job or are close enough to what you're looking for that training and development can bridge the necessary gaps.

360-degree software programs take a unique approach. They consider the customer's view! 360-degree evaluations ask sales reps to evaluate their own ability to meet customer expectations in a variety of dimensions. They also ask the sales manager and customers to evaluate the salesperson using the same criteria.

For example, given a scale of 1 to 5, with 1 representing very poor and 5 being excellent, lets say one dimension being evaluated is responsiveness to customer needs. Let's suppose that the manager rates a salesperson as a 4 on this scale. The salesperson may also evaluate himself as a 4. They both believe the results are acceptable. Just suppose the average rating of all the customers surveyed winds up at 1.3! Something needs to be done to make corrections. The salesperson and manager need to find out what has to happen to better satisfy the clients in this dimension and strive harder to make the necessary improvements.

You can't address issues you don't know exist!

Given the same scenario, let's assume the manager and customers both rate the salesperson as very low and the representative gives himself a high rating. The salesperson will have a hard time ignoring the evidence and will become less likely to offer transparent agreement with the necessary coaching from his manager.

When you measure performance factors, the job usually gets done. Using 360-Degree Surveys, you can gather data on individual sales reps and entire sales teams. Frequent assessments and follow-up surveys let you see if corrective actions are working!

Section 4:
Doing The Right Things...
Developmental Strategies

"Empty the coins in your purse into your mind and your mind will fill your purse with coins."

-Ben Franklin

Paul Zane Pilzer wrote in his book, *"Unlimited Wealth,"* about a theory he called "economic alchemy." If you can remember back to high school or college, we learned about a medieval chemical art intended to change base metals into gold. Alchemy, as it was called back then, never worked. But "economic alchemy," as Pilzer pointed out, can and does exist. For example, investments made in machinery begin to depreciate immediately. Investments in continued growth and development of employees actually helps them appreciate in value as measured by their ability to seek and discover more efficient and effective methods to produce results.

Salespeople who sell one million dollars a year who learn new strategies or ideas that enable them to sell two million dollars the next year have become appreciating assets. Education and training that transforms a one million dollar a year producer into a two million dollar a year producer is a perfect example of "economic alchemy." It takes a subject and applies a specific process that is duplicatable and turns something of limited value into much more.

Any improvement is valuable. Paul D. Cummings once told me that if you find a way to make sales people get one percent better every day, week, or month, you can see dramatic improvements over time.

The bad news is that the reverse is also true when it comes to results. If you have sales representatives who think they know all they need to know to do their jobs, their skills and subsequent results will begin to diminish. They will forget many of the things that at one time they did well. Even if a person's skills diminish at a rate of one percent a week, month, or year, what kind of results would you expect five or ten years down the road?

Given the choice of having employees skills improve or deteriorate, which would you prefer? Do you realize the long-term impact of that decision?

What if a representative could improve or deteriorate at a rate greater than one percent? What if all your representatives committed themselves to personal growth and development and all achieved greater results? What if all your representatives decided they knew everything they needed and shut themselves off from new ideas and strategies? You know your company's numbers ... do the math.

I'm convinced that too many companies don't realize or act on the importance of ongoing training and development. Alan Weiss, a management consultant and author of "Million Dollar Consulting," had an analogy that put things in proper perspective. He asks, "Can you picture a pro sports team that has finished a mediocre season of .500 ball announcing at a

Results or Consequences?

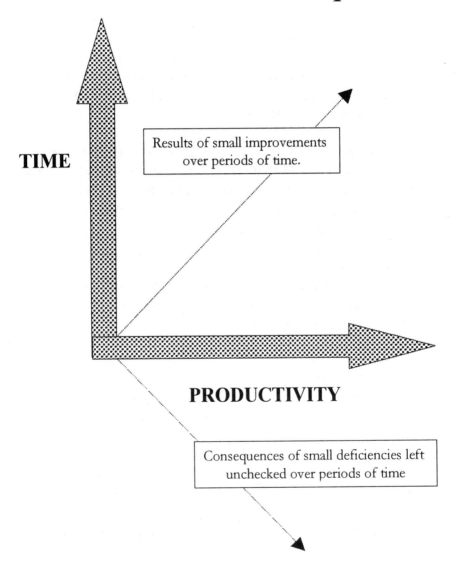

press conference ... In view of our uninspired past season, we've decided to cut back on coaching staff, reduce practice time, eliminate recruiting efforts and halve the size of the conditioning area. We think that will substantially improve our position for next year."?

The late John Hauser, undoubtedly one of the best salespeople and mentors I've ever known, once told me something that I'm going to share with you. He told me, "Growing salespeople is like planting a garden. Start with quality seeds, provide them with nourishment and give them time to grow." Then he would follow up and ask, "How would you to tend to a garden that was your only source of food?"

So I ask you, how are you tending to your only source of food? How would you describe the opportunities for professional development and training made available to salespeople through your company? Feast or famine? Are your salespeople eager to learn and develop new skills? Why or why not? What are you going to do about it?

In case you still aren't convinced that you should enhance your commitment to training and development, let's discuss dollars and sense.

Do you advertise? Why? Is it to get people to call or come by your business? Do you know the cost of a lead? If not, simply add up the cost of your annual advertising expenses and divide it by the number of prospective customers who call or come by your business. What does it cost you a year to have salespeople blowing leads they could have sold because of inadequate skills?

Kirk Mooney, a general sales manager for several radio stations in the St. Louis metropolitan area, told me a story about a large mobile home dealer who all of a sudden quit advertising on his stations. He stopped in to see why. The owner was complaining that "none of the people who came in because they heard the ads on the radio ever bought anything." While Kirk was listening to the owner, a prospective customer came in asking about a particular mobile home on the lot. The salesperson didn't leave the counter, introduce himself or even offer to help. He took the key off the wall and threw it to the prospective customer and yelled "Take a look!" Clearly it wasn't the advertising that failed to work. It was the salesperson.

Do you recognize the actual cost of a sales call for a salesperson in your company? It's easy. Add up the total cost to put the average salesperson in the field for a year. Consider salary, commissions, bonuses, benefits, marketing materials, travel and entertainment, expense reimbursements, overhead, and all other operating costs to support this person. Now divide that dollar amount by the number of appointments the average salesperson handles in a year. The results may shock you.

Costs in the hundreds of dollars per call shouldn't be a surprise. Now, when you consider the investment your company makes to send a representative on an appointment, is there any reason you wouldn't want to make sure he or she is going to be effective?

Effective Options For Enhancing Knowledge And Skills

Whatever combinations of the following methods you choose to use to educate and develop your sales staff, keep a few things in mind. A developmental program that works and continues to work must have several components. Ideally, there must be an educational support system put in place that meets your standards for both quality and quantity information. Information should be derived from only the most credible sources using a variety of methods. This information must be reinforced by repetitive exposures and continued commitment to personal and professional growth.

Your company's leadership must lead by example. It is unrealistic to expect salespeople to invest their time and money in developing their skills if their leadership doesn't set the example. Your sales staff will do what their leaders do, not what their leaders say!

Let's discuss some of the sources of quality information that are available to you.

Seminars:

This is one of the most obvious and common sources of quality information. They offer you the ability to access leading edge concepts and strategies that have produced results. You gain perspectives that might otherwise have come to light through costly trial and error. You can learn vicariously through the successes and failures of others whose ambitions and challenges are similar to yours. Get new ideas and save yourself and your company years of hard work, frustration—and potentially hundreds of thousands of dollars!

Seminars can also serve to reinforce concepts and strategies that you as a leader have shared with your sales team. If you tell a representative something, that representative may or may not believe all you've said. When your guidance is reinforced by the authority of an outside expert, your credibility goes up and your sales team is more likely to accept what you tell them.

How frustrating is it to those of you with kids when you tell them things you know will make their lives easier and they don't listen? Kids waste time, money, and opportunity but go ahead and do things "their way"—only to find out that their parents were right all along.

Why should kids listen to their parents? Is it because their parents have had the benefits of knowledge, wisdom, and judgment gained by experience and exposure to situations and challenges that their kids can't even begin to appreciate? It's for those same reasons that you and your sales staff should seek out proven experts in your field. Learn all you can from them. You already know what you know. Go find out what you don't know. Don't think you have to do it "your way." You're not a kid anymore!

There are two types of people who attend seminars. Some people are looking for a few laughs, a good meal, an excuse to get out of work for a day or two. At most, they hope for a short term burst of inspiration or one good idea. They may or may not even take notes. They have a place in their house where they put all seminar books that aren't touched until they get a new seminar book to add to the top of the pile. What a waste!

The other type are those who attend seminars, listen intently, take notes vigorously, and regularly study what they learned. In fact, not only do they study the strategies, techniques, and tactics they learned, but they rewrite, customize, and apply what they were taught in the context of their business. Then they practice, refine, and implement what they learned until they master it.

If you want to use seminars as part of your professional development program, here's some food for thought. They aren't inexpensive. Expect to invest a few hundred dollars or more, per person, for a good one. Keep in mind that there are additional expenses involved in travel, lodging, and the opportunity costs of not being at work. Another problem is that good seminars are so few and far in between that you have to rely on the discipline of your salespeople to continually review the information they gained at the last one. This may or may not happen depending on their outlook toward seminars.

The advantages you have if you know where each individual on your sales team needs improvement are numerous. First of all, you don't need to take people out of the field to send them to seminars on topics where they don't need help. Let's say a fifty person sales team attends a seminar on time management. What if only ten of them are currently struggling because of poor time management. You just wasted one day of salaries and overhead for forty people, not to mention the revenue they could have generated in the field! Furthermore the forty who didn't need to be there feel they are wasting their time and begin to feel that a corporate commitment to training and development is holding them back. Those types of feelings don't strengthen commitment to continual improvement!

Books:

Books can allow you and your sales staff to access huge quantities of quality information. Learning from books can be done without interfering with work. Exceptional representatives will read on their "free time," but I don't realistically expect everyone else will do the same. What I do think is realistic is to get everybody to make use of time they normally waste during the workday. If someone takes an hour lunch break everyday and it only takes them 30 minutes to eat, the remainder of time spent reading adds up to over 100 hours a year! Think about the time your salespeople spend in waiting areas before appointments. If a salesperson waits an average of ten minutes before each appointment and they average three or four appointments a day, then that amounts to over 100 more hours a year! These two strategies combined give your salesperson over 200 hours of education a year. Over the course of a career, we're talking about thousands of hours! All else being equal, who would you expect to accomplish more?

I used to take it one step further and highlight the parts of books I thought were most helpful. I would read them onto audiocassettes so I could listen to them over and over and over until I learned the information.

You might be thinking that there is no way you could get your salespeople to do something like that. Why not? I don't know what amazes me more, the inability of salespeople to put in an honest day's work or managers' willingness to accept so much less.

Paul D. Cummings once told me that the average car salesperson spent two hours and forty-seven minutes a day doing something directly related to making a sale. He went on to say that most salespeople would achieve much greater results if they learned to work as diligently as employees at K-Mart. What he meant was that employees who work at K-Mart work the whole time they are there! They work a few hours, steadily, without stopping, then take a 15 minute break; no more, and return to work. They work steadily until lunch, without stopping. Then they take 30 minutes; no more, and go back to work. They work without stopping a few more hours and take another 15 minute break; no more, and return to work. When things are slow, they find something productive to do, always!

Why do well-compensated, professional salespeople feel it's OK to give less effort? Why do managers let them?

Audiocassettes:

You can get from audiocassettes the same information you can get from books, seminars, or videos. Audiotapes are very convenient to use and re-use. The advantage of audiocassettes is that you can turn the time your sales team spends behind the windshield driving to and from appointments into training time. If the average salesperson spends 20,000 miles on the road each year, and counting city and highway driving, averages 30 miles an hour, that's over 600 more hours of training time a year. That amounts to fifteen 40-hour work weeks per year of pure education! What if all your salespeople did the same thing! You have created a competitive advantage without interfering with what you're currently doing!

Videocassettes:

Videocassettes are another convenient and easy way to transfer valuable information. If you don't have a video library for your sales team, start one today. Instead of sending someone to a seminar they can access the information when it's convenient.

You could easily get tempted to start making people stay after hours or come in on Saturday because you don't want training to interfere with prime selling time. Big mistake! You don't want your people thinking that additional training is punishment. False neuro-associations like that, reinforced over periods of time, can destroy an otherwise healthy atmosphere toward training and education.

I'm of the opinion that the power of suggestion can work when you have a training library. For example, if a person comes in complaining that he lost a sale because they lacked negotiating skills, suggest a video or two from your library. Tell him if he wants to get better he should check out the videos and take good notes. If your sales rep takes the time to do it, then invest whatever time you wish to coach and counsel him on what he's learned. With regard to those who don't care enough about the subject to invest their time, why should they expect you to invest your time?

TPN-The Success Channel:

What happens when employees bring their personal problems to work? What happens to their job performance? What, if anything can you do about it besides hope? Companies have tried offering employee assistance programs and counseling services to employees. That is a commendable thing, but unfortunately, it's a reactive approach.

You are about to learn about one of the most powerful shifts in the field of personal and professional development. Via digital satellite television, you, your employees, and all your families can get access to world-class sales trainers, management consultants, and best-selling authors in the comfort and convenience of your own home. These experts include people like Mark Victor Hansen, who co-authored the best selling series of books entitled *"Chicken Soup For The Soul."* Other noted authors and speakers include Dr. John Gray, author of the best seller, *"Men Are From Mars, Women Are From Venus",* Les Brown, Dr. Lillian Glass, Brian Tracy and more!

In addition to business programs on topics like selling, negotiation, time management, leadership, marketing, and others designed to help people become better employees, there are programs that affect other areas of people's lives as well. Programs exist to help families in financial straits by teaching them how to manage and invest money. Programs exist to teach spouses to enhance their relationships, improve communications, and raise children with values. Programs exist to help people attain a better level of health and fitness.

If you have salespeople in remote territories or working from their homes, this channel may be what you've been waiting for. As a leader, you can refer programs to the people who need them most without the hassles or costs of sending them videos, audios, books or tickets to seminars!

The idea behind the TPN-Success Channel is that people's lives can be changed for the better if they can get access to the "life-skills" coaches who can show them how. This television station is available along with many other news, sports and entertainment channels for around a dollar a day!

Self-Engineered Programs:

Bill Prenatt, a sales manager for Allen Foods, Inc, a very progressive whole-sale food service company, shared a unique challenge with me some time ago. He felt that the seventy-five salespeople on his staff seemed to resist training from "outsiders who didn't understand their business." He had spent big money to bring in high-powered speakers for their sales conventions and just wasn't getting the type of response he wanted from his people.

He found out that within his existing sales team there were recognized peer leaders who everyone looked up to in different areas of the business. He simply identified the core competencies that existed in his industry and identified the recognized peer authorities on each of those competencies. He decided to let them be the experts because he knew the other members of the sales team would pay attention.

During one sales conference, he put together an expert panel, consisting of several top producers who in the past had worked for competitors. He let them field questions from the rest of the sales force on how to sell against competition. The sales force was actively participating in the process of gaining new knowledge, not just sitting passively. They obviously enjoyed it, and it was an outstanding success.

He simply replicated the idea at other conferences using other topics. He has since built upon the idea of self-engineered training to include customized workbooks, videocassettes and audiocassettes that give the salespeople the information they need most from people they view as credible authorities.

Mentor/Coach:

It never seems like sales managers get to spend enough time in the field with their salespeople. It just seems that there aren't enough days. Make sure your managers make the most of each day.

Knowing what you now know about the assessment tools that are available, there is no excuse for managers not to know where their people need help. Managers should be prepared to discuss ways to help the salesperson make the necessary improvements.

Have you ever become tired of telling a salesperson the same thing time and time again? Managers should insist that their salespeople bring an audiocassette player to record the constructive coaching sessions that should be taking place in between calls.

When I was brand new in sales, the appointments I went on with my boss were like vacations compared to the work that went on in between appointments. I can still hear the questions in my head ...What did you do well? What could you have done differently? Why? There was no such thing as an enjoyable drive. Drive time was work time. We talked; I learned!

Before you begin:

What can the people who work for you expect to gain by participating and doing things ordinary people wouldn't do to better themselves? What's in it for them ... personal satisfaction, higher incomes, better job security, better family life, better health, promotions, awards, recognition? Are they doing it to avoid the fear of getting fired and the pain of a career change? Are there enough reasons to keep them committed? Do you hold them accountable to themselves? To you? Do you remind them?

What can you do to continually encourage them? They may not care enough about themselves to go the extra mile, but may care enough about what you or others think of them to stick with the program! Be sure to let your people know that you notice their extra effort. Let them know you care and that they are important enough to warrant your attention.

The last words on training and development:

Just start. Do something. Any effort to acquire new skills and education beats passively watching skills erode! Don't think you need some elaborate program that you have to put together before you get going! Start the process. Build upon it until you find out what works best! Considerations that will enhance the effectiveness of any developmental efforts will include:

A) Multi-sensory learning strategies

Visual learning (Learning by seeing)

Auditory learning (Learning by hearing)

Kinesthetic learning (Learning by doing)

B) Providing information that is ...

Credible

Relevant and interesting

From a variety of sources

Convenient to access

Affordable

Reinforced by multiple exposures at spaced repetitions

Section 5:
Doing The Right Things... Strategic Decisions

I've spent time discussing what I consider to be the foundation and corner-stone of any sales driven organization committed to long term success. One word tells it all—people. Unfortunately, having the right people isn't always enough, particularly when they are held hostage by antiquated, senseless, and restrictive systems or processes that inhibit their ability to achieve excellence.

It's for that reason I wish to focus the remainder of this book on some relevant sales increasing strategies and the tactics to implement those strategies in the most efficient and cost effective means possible.

I had reached a point, not long ago, where I began to think that I was doing everything I could to grow my business both efficiently and cost effectively. I almost fell into that trap of "not messing with something that's working," thinking that I so detest in prospective clients.

Then I got a telephone call from an acquaintance who was launching a sales force consulting company as an affiliate of the Cargill Consulting Group out of California. He invited me to attend an informational briefing hosted by Mr. Gil Cargill, who has been dubbed by the media as "The Sales Doctor."

I was captivated by his ability to break down the components and fundamentals of good sales management. Cargill described his work as a way to apply Deming's approach to "Total Quality Management" in a sales management context. He had an ability to minimize the guesswork of sales management in favor of common sense decision making, based on facts, figures, and analysis.

He went on to point out that there are several key strategies a company can implement to improve results. These strategies and the order in which they should be considered are as follows:

1) Improve the "Consideration Rate": Sure your salespeople can dance … why can't they get a date? Too many salespeople never reach their full potential because they don't have enough opportunities to tell their story. Productive prospecting is more than dialing for dollars and knocking on doors. It takes more than billboards, direct mail and media advertising.

How many deals are going on in your territories that your salespeople aren't even in on? What can be done to improve your salespeople's ability to be considered as a potential supplier. Prospects can't buy products or services they don't know about from companies or salespeople they don't even know exist.

2) Increase "Sales Time": Reduce time spent on activities other than selling. How much time do your salespeople actually spend each day physically engaged in the act of selling? Time spent in planning, travel, doing paperwork or prospecting does not count. More time needs to be spent doing activities that generate revenue.

3) Decrease "Time per Transaction": How much time does a salesperson have to spend selling to make a sale? To calculate the time per transaction, simply multiply the amount of time spent with the average prospect times the closing rate.

> **For example:** Selling time spent with the average prospect = 1.5 hours
>
> Closing Ratio = 25% (4 attempts to make 1 sale)
>
> Calculation of Time Per Transaction = 1.5 X 4 = 6 selling hrs/sale

Companies have found that the profit they generate from one sale may be less than the cost to support the sales time needed to acquire that sale. Knowing this figure can let your company know if it is heading for an eventual disaster!

4) Increase "Revenue per Transaction": How much revenue will each sale generate? It is calculated by dividing gross sales revenue by the number of transactions.

Your company could be pursuing market segments that generate relatively low "Revenue per Transaction" and take just as long and cost just as much to acquire as bigger clients. If that's the case, perhaps you should target your markets differently or find ways of reducing costs to acquire clients in that market segment. You might also seek ways to increase the revenue generated through your existing client base with add-on sales of similar or related products or services.

Your company may also be ignoring the lifetime value of that customer and failing to invest properly in maintaining that client relationship. A $9,000 per year account translates to $90,000 over ten years and $180,000 over twenty years. That's not even including the additional revenue generated from referrals given by the satisfied client.

5) **"Increase the number of salespeople":** Many people immediately think that adding salespeople is an easy way to gain marketshare. In most cases, I agree, provided that appropriate business practices and support systems are in place to implement the strategies and tactics discussed in this book.

The necessity of adding new salespeople in numerous sales environments has diminished greatly thanks to technology. A sales territory that used to support ten salespeople using traditional sales strategies and tactics might only be able to support half that sales force if you put in place technology and systems that double productivity.

• **Free Bonus Offer-** If you don't want to do the math, that's OK. Call us and we will be happy to help you. We have a computer program that will calculate these ratios to help you determine things like: Annual Selling Hours per Person, Maximum Number of Transactions per Year (per Person or per Team), Maximum Dollars/Year (per Person or per Team), Revenue per Sales Hour and more! This program will also give you the ability to perform "what-if" calculations and estimate the potential incremental revenue you can expect to gain from implementing each strategy. We will be happy to perform this analysis free of charge. Just contact us and mention that you heard about us in this book!

Let me give you a practical example of how you can use those figures to improve your decision-making abilities.   Just suppose that your average salesperson generates $10,000 a week in sales revenue but only spends an average of ten hours per week actually engaged in the act of selling. That means every person in your sales organization earns your company $1,000 during every hour they spend selling. My next question is an obvious one. Are your salespeople spending the time that yields $1,000 per hour doing things you could pay someone else hourly wages to accomplish? What are those activities? Identify and reassign them. You may be surprised to see what the status quo is costing you.

That's just one example of applying the concept of "Revenue per Sales Hour." The other figures can also provide valuable insights into your sales and marketing decisions. Once you have the data you need, you can make sound, educated decisions on which of these strategies to implement. You can also decide on the order in which they should be implemented.

Determining strategies is one thing; knowing how to implement them is another. With the right tools and tactics, implementation can be much easier for you than it is for others!

Before I introduce you to a few of my favorite strategies, let me urge precaution regarding the use of technology.

Mr. Gene Mace, the CEO of the U.S. Media Group shared an interesting story. I'll share it with you. The U.S. Media Group owns and manages numerous small-market newspapers all over the country. They are notorious for taking over failing newspapers and turning them around. Quickly.

Evidently, one of his publishers had put together a thorough and convincing proposal for the purchase of an expensive new type of printing press that he believed would dramatically enhance productivity, and wanted to secure funds to make the purchase. He informed Mr. Mace that the improved productivity could easily justify the purchase price.

Mr. Mace asked the publisher which employees he was going to terminate since this new press could obviously do the job with fewer people. "Nobody, I'll just find something else for them to do," he replied. Mr. Mace quickly informed him that if there was other work that needed to be done around the newspaper, he should have hired someone to fill those positions. He went on to inform his publisher that his job wasn't to make worker's jobs easier. His job was to make a profit. The publisher decided to keep the existing employees and the existing press.

The reason I shared this story is simple. Some of the technologies and strategies you will read about have increased the productivity of some sales organizations by several times.

One of my clients in the printing industry implemented so effectively some of the ideas I'm about to share, that his firm outgrew its capacity to deliver everything their salespeople could sell! Keep in mind, those are great problems to have, but new technology, strategies, and tactics make more choices and options available. Choose wisely!

- You can maintain your current level of success in half the time you're spending now.

- Your team can become twice as productive. In other words, you can make twice as much money.

- You can experience a combination of both.

Section 6:
Achieving Maximum
Levels of Sales Productivity

In the face of unprecedented competition, many companies have invested tens of thousands of dollars in laptop computers, e-mail systems, wide area networks, internet connectivity, and contact management software. The goal of these acquisitions was not merely to provide state-of-the-art technology, but rather to increase sales and reduce expenses, thereby improving profitability.

In most cases, the results of sales force automation have been dismally disappointing. **Technology increased—sales did not.**

It has been our experience that most companies do not have a clear picture of what it is that they want technology to accomplish when they initiate a sales force automation project. Nor do they have an understanding of the concept of "appropriate technology."

To help clarify the key issues, this section will discuss the tactics and strategies of effective prospecting, cross marketing, and client retention. Our goal is to explain what we have found to be the most effective way of selling any product or service that has a long sales cycle or is "relationship based." These strategies are especially effective if your product is a considered a large or expensive purchase.

First the basics.

The challenge of the next decade is to be in front of prospects when they are ready to buy, not when you're ready to sell.

Let's talk about how proper use of technology can be a tactical advantage for your sales team in implementing the above strategies and managing the sales process. Please notice that I said manage the sales "process," not the sales "person."

Sales is a process in some ways not that different from the manufacturing process. For example, let's say your company manufactures chairs. You start with raw materials that go through specific steps in a specific order to create the finished product. If you were to rearrange or delete any steps in the process, you would end up with junk.

Sales also has a process. Specific steps exist that can:

- Introduce your company to prospects

- Turn customers into referral sources

- Transform uninterested prospects into customers through education and follow up contact

- Educate customers on other products or services

Once you have determined the most effective and efficient processes, you can begin to look for ways to automate those steps, wherever possible. Let me give you some food for thought as you look for ways to define your processes and set up systems to implement them.

Computers can be your best friend or worst enemy. The difference is in who controls the process. I suggest that you are better off having your salespeople sell, your administrators handle clerical tasks, and your customer service and support personnel supporting whenever possible. **Let salespeople sell.** We have clients using a centralized marketing approach where it only takes 1 or 2 administrative support people to manage the entire sales and marketing activities for 50 salespeople. The salespeople make phone calls, see prospects, and put out fires with customers that only they can handle.

Why So Many Salespeople Never Become Top Producers

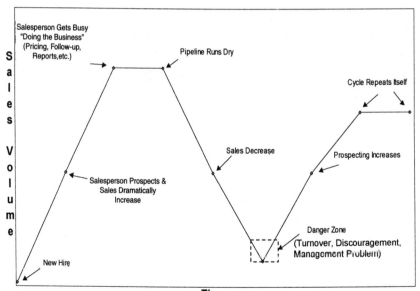

© PS LLC 1999

It's been my experience that salespeople come in two types, "Hunters" and "Farmers." Both types can possess that "As long as I'm on quota, stay out of my way, don't bother me with details, call reports or forecasts" mentality.

Hunters live for the thrill of the chase of the new account and lose interest as soon as their commission check clears. They would rather look for new customers then spend time with their existing clients. Unfortunately, winning prizes, trips and awards only reinforces their losing behavior. They don't realize that getting customers is the first step and that keeping them is an ongoing process. Eventually, they leave for the next "great opportunity" and leave their manager with a pile of dead end leads—leads with no background information or follow up.

On the other hand, farmers never leave. They baby and coddle their customers. They almost never lose clients, but they don't ever make time to get new ones! The Farmer's micro-managing is just as detrimental in the long term as the Hunter's lack of caring. He keeps records on every client and every imaginable detail. This is the last guy you want to have a computer! It would become an unlimited, unfillable file box. It would grow and grow until it took over his existence. Information is only useful if it brings you closer to your goal.

It's a balancing act. When reps are selling, performing their service or delivering their product, they aren't prospecting. It's always one or the other and reps under traditional methods conclude that they can't do it all at once. When you finish this book, you will see that's not the case!

The obvious problem is this: prospects and customers take time. Who has that much time? Nobody. Unless, that is, they have an automated data base marketing system that compiles and organizes tasks and reports in an orderly manner and is relentless in its pursuit of prospecting activities and customer retention.

Properly developed systems will know every customer's birthday, anniversary, product likes and dislikes. It will know how much customers buy, how often they buy and at what price. Properly developed systems are also proactive enough to contact potential and current clients with little or no effort on the part of the salesperson and introduce them to products and services that fit their needs.

Companies touting sales automation usually come from two schools of thought. The first group includes computer and software companies. Because of the nature of their business and what they produce, their number one goal has to be—sell the largest volume of computer hardware and software possible. Their way of thinking insists that everyone in every office needs a computer and a whole library of software to go with it.

By profession, most hardware and software vendors are computer engineers and technical types. They don't and probably won't ever understand sales. Many "techies" don't have complimentary things to say about sales departments.

So ... they have two strikes against them:

1. They have a vested interest in volume sales of their software and equipment.

2. They don't know anything about sales and marketing. It's like asking a blind barber if you need a haircut ... then trusting him to do a good job.

At the other end of the spectrum, there are traditional marketing consultants. They may understand sales, but they only have ideas to sell. Most companies need a proven action plan and a system for managing it. In addition, marketing consultants are relatively new to the automation field. Are you ready to serve as the guinea pig on which some consultant is going to test his newest brainstorm?

The problem with sales automation is not with the concept—it's in the development, the overall strategy, and the follow-up support.

It's been my experience that too many sales force automation projects fail despite everyone's good intentions. Failing efforts are characterized by salespeople transformed into overpriced data entry clerks. They try to manage the details necessary for success and spend their time in front of computer screens, not prospects who can sign checks!

Lets talk about the companies that do succeed in automating their sales and marketing functions. Developing and implementing systems for hundreds of companies has taught us several truths. I'm going to share them with you.

Successful marketing strategies and tactics must include the following elements:

1. Sales efforts must be targeted to a specific market that is "predisposed" to investing in your product or service. Mass marketing through non-directed advertising is both ineffective and expensive.

2. The strategy must clearly state a unique selling proposition. This means that a unique customer oriented benefit must be effectively and persuasively presented to the prospect. This benefit must state clearly why the product or service is superior to all others in the market and what benefit(s) the customer should expect to receive as a result of investing his capital.

3. All communication must be personalized and directed specifically to the decision makers and influencers.

4. Any successful strategy must be methodical. Most customer/prospect contact is sporadic, poorly timed, and inconsistent. "One-shot" advertising, sales letters and telephone calls do not provide the necessary consistency for any effective sales effort.

5. All successful marketing campaigns require that follow up be systematic, organized, and provide management with necessary reports to monitor sales performance. The management adage that states "you cannot man-

age what you cannot see" is especially true in sales and marketing management.

Every Company That Sells A Product Or Service Has Several Problems Or Challenges In Common:

1. Sales is either a process or a problem. Most companies don't have an effective strategy of consistent, professional, and targeted prospect contact for the purpose of building market share or increasing incremental revenue from their existing client base.

2. Unsolicited telephone calls are considered intrusive and unprofessional.

3. Most advertising isn't targeted and doesn't cause the prospect to take any immediate action.

4. Initial sales calls are expensive and time consuming. The more remote the territory, the more the expense incurred.

5. Sales professionals are difficult to manage. It's more effective to manage the sales process.

6. Conditions within companies are dynamic. This means that the prospect who was not interested last quarter could be today.

7. Statistically, eighty percent of all sales are booked after the fifth contact, yet the majority of salespeople give up after the second contact.

8. Most salespeople aren't involved in enough selling opportunities to exceed sales goals.

9. Selling cycles are getting longer. Salespeople must be prepared to stay In contact with prospects over an extended period of time.

10. As product differentiation becomes more difficult, prospects base buying decisions on relationships with vendors perceived to be the most

professional and service oriented.

11. Customers must be nurtured and continually reminded of their importance to the company. In fact, studies have shown that over forty percent of customers "fire" vendors they think don't care!

All selling and marketing efforts can be simplified into the following four steps:

1. Identify a prospect.

2. Introduce the prospect to your products and services.

3. Cultivate the prospect through follow-up activities.

4. Close the sale when the prospect is ready to buy.

Clearly, step three is the "Achilles Heel" in many sales organizations. The most common reasons why salespeople don't follow-up well are:

1. **They don't like to.** There are many salespeople who are great at prospecting, presenting, and closing, but fail to maintain contact through repeated visits or letter writing.

2. **They are too busy.** Many salespeople are focused on short-term opportunities and feel they can't spend the time to cultivate long-term relationships.

3. **They are not well organized and lose track of when to follow up.** Some salespeople allow things to pile up and have no system to remind them when it's time to get back in touch with someone.

4. **They leave the territory and no one else continues their efforts.** When a new salesperson takes over a territory, transition efforts usually focus on the "good" customers. Any prospects the prior salesperson was cultivating are frequently dropped. Sometimes, if the old salesperson leaves

the company, he or she continues to cultivate the prospects (for your competition).

5. **There is no formal plan as to how prospects and customers are to be cultivated.** Most organizations have never developed a plan for follow-up. If they have, it's typically not well managed.

In an attempt to address these issues, companies are beginning to use computers and contact management software. While this may help a few salespeople become more productive, it still won't achieve the desired results. The problems I just listed remain. Each salesperson manages his own plan as he sees fit, not as management does. Poorly organized salespeople who couldn't manage a day planner still let things pile up. When reps leave the company, copies of the data go with them and the sales manager ends up trying to put together a picture of a territory that looks like a puzzle with half the pieces missing.

To achieve the desired results a system must address each of the problems listed earlier by meeting the following design objectives:

1. **The system must have a formal plan.** Management must design a plan and specific processes that dictate how, when and what prospect follow-up is to occur. The system must automatically manage the activities for each prospect, assuring that nothing and no one "falls through the cracks." Letters and reports for all salespeople must be automatically produced without any prodding by individual salespeople.

This plan should consist of strategies that include alternative channels of contact. Make sure your plan has a combination of advertising, targeted mailings, timely phone calls, and face to face visits with prospects. Someone who has his mail screened may take phone calls or listen to voice mail messages. Others may not take calls unless they have seen information in advance. Let me encourage you to develop a system that will satisfy almost anybody.

The costs of physical sales calls are the most expensive channel of contact and should be used on your best sales opportunities where the probability of success is high. They average a few hundred dollars each, depending on your industry. If eighty percent of all sales don't happen until after the fifth contact and many don't happen until after the tenth or fifteenth, you could be looking at an extremely high cost of acquiring new clients if you rely on that channel alone.

It is difficult to justify the cost of sending a salesperson to make a face to face presentation unless the prospect is both highly qualified and highly interested. Levels of interest can be increased with a strategic marketing plan and effective, alternative channels of contact. By qualified, I mean that a potential customer:

A) Can make a decision

B) Has a need that can be met by your product or service

C) Can afford to buy.

In addition to being qualified, the prospect must also be interested. Interested in you, your company, and your solutions. The ideal prospect is someone who is highly qualified and very interested. Without both elements in place, your salesperson is wasting his or her time.

Determining who is qualified is a key part of "selling on purpose," but the prospect's interest level is often a matter of timing. The prospect who is not interested today may be very interested tomorrow, next week, or two quarters from now. The problem is that unless you have a process for staying in touch with qualified prospects, someone else will "harvest your crop." To define who is qualified and implement a process of increasing the prospect's interest through a systematic process is called – **Magic!!!** Later in this section we will show you how this can work for your company.

Top producers spend their time, their only non-renewable resource, with prospects that meet both criteria.

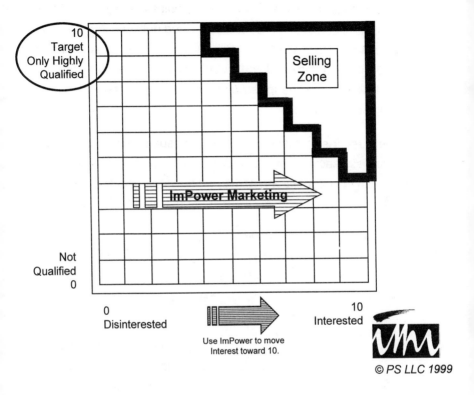

© PS LLC 1999

2. The system must be centralized. In a centralized system, one person, or a small group of people, clerical in nature, can be responsible for managing the database marketing system. Using a centralized system you can achieve consistency in your treatment of all prospects regardless of which salesperson is working with them. In addition, prospecting activities are also protected against disruption during the transition to a new salesperson. Any contact scheduled with the prospect will continue automatically.

3. Management reporting must be timely and provide useful information. Managers must know on a "real-time" basis if salespeople are not making their sales calls. If you have no means of knowing what your salespeople are or are not doing (other than taking their word for it), you will be taken advantage of. Unfortunately, too many sales managers put their credibility on the line for salespeople who aren't working hard—if they're working at all!

Management reports can also let you measure the quality of your lead sources, success securing appointments, closing percentages and more so that you can adjust your approaches, set realistic forecasts, and budget accordingly.

A large banking client was regretting the expenditure of $1,000,000 (yes, six zeros!) on billboards throughout their market area. Was it successful? Was it a waste of money? They didn't know. They had no way of tracking the success or failure of their marketing campaign. (P.S.-They do now.)

Another client used trade shows to generate leads. Their problem was that the salespeople refused to call the leads. Why? They were so old by the time they were shipped from the main office to the branches and finally distributed to the sales reps that they weren't any good.

With proper management reporting, sales managers don't have to baby-sit, plead, or nag! No more ... What did you do today?—Who did you call on today?—Why were you in the office all day?—Why weren't you in the office all day today?

Prospecting is not a matter of luck. It is not just catching a prospect who happens to be interested in buying your product or service. Nor is it a matter of getting your foot in the door and talking as fast as you can, hoping to catch someone's interest.

Prospecting is a science that allows your salespeople to "harvest" prospects that are ready to buy now and to "cultivate" those that aren't ready yet. Research shows that most sales are not made on the first contact. As pointed out earlier, eighty percent of sales are made after the fifth contact. Unfortunately, most sales people quit after the first or second try. They suffer from the "I'm ready to sell. Are you ready to buy?" syndrome.

What happens to the eighty percent of prospects that are qualified to buy your products or services but just aren't ready now? Salespeople are paid for the sales they make today and cannot afford to invest energy in a sale that may be six months to a year away.

Meanwhile, your company is losing the opportunity to sell to the eighty percent who aren't ready today. Unlike an individual salesperson, your company can afford to wait another six months for a sales opportunity to mature. The question is how much is the neglected eighty percent affecting your bottom line now? What about next quarter ... or next year?

How can your company or organization address the issue of focusing on only the low hanging fruit - the opportunities that are ripe today? You need a system that oversees the entire sales cycle. A system that introduces new prospects to your organization involves a salesperson only when prospects have expressed an interest to buy now. A system that continues to stay in contact after the sale insures repeat business. It does no good to attract five new clients only to have six walk out the back door due to neglect.

The current wisdom says, "If I give each of my salespeople the best tools, my sales force will become more productive." The best tools usually means an expensive computer and contact management software. Our experience with sales organizations has proven that if a sales person won't keep up a $50 day planner, he or she won't be more productive with a $3000 computer! In fact, just the opposite is true. Without a plan or system, a computer can add just one more complicated layer to the sales cycle.

Does this mean sales force automation is a bad idea? No. In fact, a well-designed, automated, sales and marketing system can increase sales and improve customer retention. But only if it is properly implemented.

First, the difference between sales and marketing needs to be understood. To explain the difference, a garden or farm offers the best analogy. Marketing is about preparing the soil, planting the seeds, and nurturing the fragile plants. Selling is about harvesting.

Too often we ask our sales people to find the gardens of others and harvest crops where they haven't planted. Fortunately, there is a more productive way to increase sales—a prospecting and marketing system.

It is the responsibility of marketing to identify the opportunities, organize advertising, develop fulfillment packages, and get the crop ready for harvest. Then, the job of sales is to go out and pick the ripe, low hanging fruit after a relationship has been cultivated.

A sales and marketing system makes it possible to effectively oversee every aspect of sales, marketing, and territory management. By using the power and intelligence of a computer, you can map out in advance a total marketing plan. This centralized system can be managed by a single marketing coordinator or gatekeeper. The good news is that a system solution is less expensive and more effective than allowing each individual to manage his or her marketing and prospecting efforts. A marketing strategy is not limited to business and commercial use. Marketing systems have been successfully implemented by schools, non-profit organizations, and a wide range of commercial businesses. Organizations with a sales force, staff, or a group of volunteers find that they can accomplish much more with limited resources than those without a system.

Developing a successful system is as simple as defining a beginning point and separating the process of selling into discrete steps. Map out on a flowchart all of the possibilities and program the system to generate the correspondence, fulfillment packages, and reports that should drive the fund raiser, membership drive, or marketing campaign.

Such a system emphasizes the importance of your company's values regarding it's products and services and their relationship to your customers. More importantly, through the system you work at developing customers and; as a result, earn the sales you make. Sales are no longer just "check marks" on a manager's chalkboard, but a testament of your organization's commitment to creating and keeping customers for life.

Why You Need To Systematize Your Sales Process

The gap between the most successful sales teams and those struggling to achieve can be traced to a very small difference. Consider the impact of one additional phone call per day, one extra appointment per week, one more referral per month or an additional group presentation per quarter. The challenge is to consistently do the little extras that make the difference between mediocrity and top performance.

Salespeople and their managers tell us every day that they know what to do:

- Prospect

- Get referrals

- Network with other professionals

- Read continuously and stay on top of the industry

- Send a personal thank you letter to every new client

- Say thank you for every referral

- Cross-sell established customers

- Develop new territories and selling opportunities.

The question is—How can you find the time and resources to do everything you already know you should be doing? If you also have a sales team to manage, multiply your tasks by the number of people you supervise.

Sales managers are at the nerve center. They're expected to make the forecasts and still cater to everyone's agenda. It's a difficult job without good tools. After working with several hundred sales teams, we have developed an eight-step process for sales and territory management.

This proven process increases productivity, serves customers better, and allows managers to coach, not coerce, their associates.

Step One - Define the territory

Determine where you want to do business. Territories can be geographic, assigned accounts or vertical markets. Make a map of where your prospects are located. It could be a number of miles from your office or within easy flying distance for day trips.

Step Two - Select prospects within your territory.

Decide who buys what you sell and then build a profile of your ideal prospect. What does this company look like? What industry segment or profession do they represent? Does the target own the company or is your most qualified buyer a senior level executive? Does the net worth or level of annual income matter?

Make a list of the requirements for your perfect prospect. If you have several ideal prospects, make a separate list or profile for each. This process will ensure that you spend time, your only nonrenewable resource, with qualified prospects.

Step Three - Build the database of qualified buyers.

Your goal is to build a database of qualified prospects located in your territory. Remember the Qualified and Interested chart? Your goal is to make

ImPower Marketing
The Eight Step Selling Process

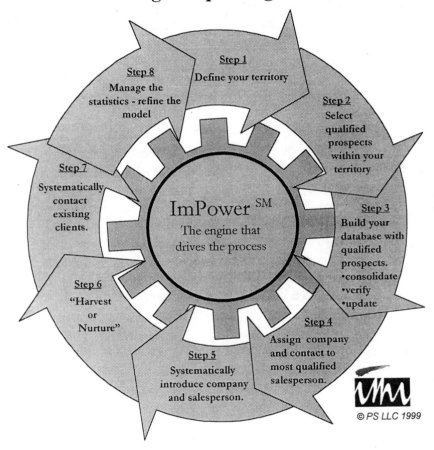

© PS LLC 1999

sure that anyone in your database falls in the eight to ten range on the chart. This list should consist of the following:

- Active prospects

- Old customers you would like to get back

- Names you should be calling on but haven't gotten to yet

- Referral sources

- Commercial lists (typically purchased) and organization lists.

Classic database marketing usually ends at this point. Mass mailings or campaigns are often launched with typical results of a .5 to 2 percent return. Those who are not ready to purchase right now are often lost as a sales opportunity.

With a hit-and-miss sales effort, the last person in the door often gets the order. The problem is that **you paid** for marketing and educating the prospect, but you didn't **get paid** for the sale.

Step Four: Assign a field associate to every client and prospect.

A successful sales or marketing program depends on consistent, persistent, and personal contact. Without a systematic process, you're throwing darts in the dark, hoping against hope that something will stick and a sale can be made.

We all buy from people we know and have confidence in. You can't build rapport with "Dear Occupant" or "Dear Sir." Even the most clever marketing campaign loses effectiveness unless it's personalized.

Every person in your database should be assigned to an associate for accountability and for that "personal touch."

Step Five - Systematically introduce your company and associates to every person in the database.

Over time, every person in your database should be educated about your organization and introduced to the associate assigned to him or her. Using your perfect prospect profile as a guide, make a list of individuals and/or companies, and include them in your marketing strategy.

Plan to build prospect interest systematically through alternative channels of communication. Using a combination of personal letters, faxes, information packets, e-mails, phone calls, and personal visits, stay in front of prospects until **they are ready to buy!**

When the process is done correctly, prospects will call you when they are ready to buy because you have taken the time to introduce yourself, to educate them over time and to stay with them.

Here is an illustration of how important it is to contact qualified prospects consistently.

Most sales are made after the eighth contact. Most salespeople quit calling after only two calls. Persistence pays when it comes to building a customer base. By your eighth contact, you may be the only one left in the game. Your chances of being called when someone wants to buy are about ninety percent. That's the kind of leverage that makes a strategy successful.

The question is, how can any individual producer, sales team or company find the time to cultivate and maintain the number of contacts necessary to stay in the game? Associates are compensated to find people who are ready to buy today They are not necessarily motivated to nurture prospects through a long-term sales cycle. There is nothing more discouraging than finding out a day late about a selling opportunity. Not to be chosen is one thing—not to even be considered is disheartening.

Develop a long-term sales strategy that maps out your sales cycle in advance and leaves nothing to chance. Start with an actual diagram or flowchart of your sales cycle. Quiz yourself repeatedly about the "what ifs." If this happens, what is the logical next step or steps? Then, fill in all of the blanks with the appropriate responses. For example, if you get a referral, what do you want to happen next? I suggest that a letter of introduction go out mentioning the person who gave you the referral. The letter should followed by a reminder to call and personally introduce yourself—the personal touch. What if you don't get an appointment right away? Decide how you can stay in touch until the prospect is ready to meet with you.

The person who gave you the lead should get a thank-you letter or gift. Then, next quarter, you can request additional referrals.

The goal is to plan ahead and never let opportunities fall through the "cracks." The best sales and marketing systems take the day-to-day details of marketing out of the hands of the salespeople, thus creating time for them to make presentations and close business. Most good salespeople are not detail oriented, and their time is better spent in the field than in front of a computer.

We have found that a central administrator or "gatekeeper" can manage the efforts of an entire sales force and do a much better job of staying in touch. Sales reps can be notified when someone needs attention.

Step Six - Close business that is ready now but have a process in place to "nurture" those that are not ready now.

As you work through your list of ideal prospects, some will be ready to buy right now. Make the sale. A system should never be an excuse to put off doing business today. Use your charted sales cycle to determine what's next. Send a proposal, say thank you, follow up, and ask for a referral. Always be prepared to manage the next step so that nothing gets left to chance or inadvertently ignored. Move the new client into the next phase of your sales process; cross selling.

Step Seven - Systematically contact existing clients.

Have you ever had a client say to you, **"I didn't know you did that."?** If you have, then you have a cross-marketing problem. Many companies have loyal clients who are buying from competitors simply because they are not aware of their entire product or service offerings.

Our work with one large insurance company identified more than 20,000 orphaned and neglected clients in just one region. None of these customers had been contacted by an agent within the past five years, and for some it had been twenty years. These loyal customers just kept paying their premium. The question is: How many other policies did they purchase from other companies during the same time period? A lot of additional business was allowed to go somewhere else because of neglect.

This problem is not confined to the insurance industry. Virtually every client that we work with has admitted that customers frequently were unaware of everything they sold.

By arranging your marketing strategy to include a cross marketing plan, you can dramatically improve your sales and profits. The old adage that it makes more sense to keep a customer than to try to find a new one could not be more accurate.

Remember: — The goal of sales process management is to manage the sales cycle, not the salesperson.

Step Eight - Refine, correct, and repeat.

After the first year you should have enough information to start charting and graphing your results. You will start seeing trends. If the trend is good, you will have the tools and knowledge to do more of the same. You will be able to find more prospects that fit your success profile, expand into other territories, or discover new niche markets. If you don't like the results in a given strategy area, you will have the information you need to make corrections and improve your selling process. Now you can stop doing what isn't working and spend those resources in areas that you know are effective. But until you establish a company standard, you can't track variations. Your system will establish a baseline for tracking results.

Sales is now and will always be a numbers game. The new leaders in the industry have adopted a systematic approach to territory management that covers all bases. A system can get business moving your way and give you the edge you need to win.

I've been talking somewhat vaguely about sales processes and computerized database marketing systems to implement them. Let me be more specific. Depending on the size of your company, it's possible to run your entire sales and marketing plan from one PC or PC network, supported by, at most, a few support personnel. It's possible to utilize extremely flexible software that can be customized to meet your needs.

A complete sales and marketing process will be comprised of several sub-processes or "modules." These modules will be comprised of activity sequences; typically combinations of letters, phone calls, and face to face visits that move a prospect toward the sale. The content should vary based on your company's message and target market, but many of the basics are the same.

1. Basic Prospecting Module—should include:

A) Introductory marketing messages- usually letters, spaced at least five to seven days apart, that introduce your company, your products, and your salesperson

B) Introduction to a referral letter

C) Response letter to a request for information

D) Call Back, Reminder & Management reports to ensure follow up and completion of above approaches.

2. Prospect Nurturing Modules – get prospects to call you when they are ready to buy:

A) An "After The Appointment Follow-up Series" should educate prospects about your industry.

B) A "Wait-Series" keeps in touch with prospects that weren't necessarily disinterested, but didn't feel the timing was right. It maintains "Top Of The Mind Awareness" and keeps potential clients from falling through the cracks.

C) Call Back, Reminder & Management reports ensure follow up and completion of above approaches.

3. Client Maintenance Modules –

A) Thank new customers for their orders.

B) Survey customers for quality control purposes.

C) Maintain on-going client contact so customers don't feel neglected.

D) Call Back, Reminder & Management reports ensure follow up and completion of above approaches.

4. Cross-marketing modules introduce clients to other products and services.

5. Trade Show, Special Event, and Seminar Series modules:

A) Manage invitations and follow-up from seminars, trade shows, or special events.

B) Track and respond to birthdays, anniversaries, and other special data.

Let's examine the basics of a sample sales process and take a look at how to tie it all together. Before we begin, let's assume that we have a salesperson with a defined territory and a database full of prospects deemed qualified. We have a system administrator who is responsible for printing, folding, signing, stuffing, and mailing all letters. He is also in charge of data entry and data exchange between the computer, salesperson, and sales manager by means of various call reports. That being said ... let's get into it.

This will be a portion of a scenario for handling new prospects. For this example, we will address prospects which meet the following conditions:

1. We have never had contact with them before.

2. We do not have a referral to them.

3. They have not contacted us.

Before we call on one of these prospects, we want to send a series of three short letters, five days apart, to create some basic familiarity with our company, our products, services and with the salesperson who will be calling them. Five days after the last letter, we want the salesperson to receive a report indicating what has transpired and announcing that it is time to contact the prospect. This sequence can be defined as follows:

Scenario Segment 1: New Prospects as Follows			
♦ We have never had contact with them before. ♦ We do not have a referral to them. ♦ They have not contacted us.			
Here we wish to send 3 introductory letters and then prepare a salesperson action report.			
Event	Description	Next Event	Days
1	Introductory Letter #1	2	5
2	Introductory Letter #2	3	5
3	Introductory Letter #3	20	5
20	Sales Rep Action Report	21	5
21	Mgmt. Exception Report	21	5

Once we have created our Marketing Scenario, we must write the letters and create the report format. Any time we start a contact on Event #1, the system will print our first letter on Day #1, our second letter on Day #6, our third letter on Day #11. On Day #16 a report will be printed for the salesperson instructing him to call the prospect.

What we really want to happen is for the salesperson to make contact with the prospect and then to make a decision regarding the appropriate course of action to be followed next. To accomplish this, we will create four alternative scenarios which can be followed.

Alternative 1:	The Prospect is interested in meeting and we set an appointment.		
Here we wish to send an appointment confirmation letter immediately and then create another Salesperson Action Report which indicates the appointment.			
Event	**Description**	**Next Event**	**Days**
30	Appt. Confirmation Letter	31	0
31	Salesperson Action Report	3	5

Alternative 2:	The prospect is not willing to see us now, but may be interested at some point in the future.		
Here we want to send a thank you letter indicating that we will be back in touch in the future. When the time arrives, we want to send a letter reminding the prospect that we will be calling him, based upon our prior conversation. Finally, we want to prepare a Salesperson Action Report.			
Event	**Description**	**Next Event**	**Days**
40	Thank You - I'll Be In Touch	41	Future
41	Will Be Calling-As You Asked	20	5
20	Salesperson Action Report		

Alternative 3:	The prospect is not interested and absolutely never will be...		
Here we want to send a letter thanking him for his time and ask him for referrals.			
Event	**Description**	**Next Event**	**Days**
50	Thank You – Tell Others		

Alternative 4: The prospect is not taking our calls or returning them.

Here we wish to send a letter saying that we understand he's been busy and we've been unable to reach him. We ask him to be expecting our call or to call us if it's more convenient. After that, we prepare a Salesperson Action Report and try again.

Event	Description	Next Event	Days
60	No Contact Letter-Please Call	20	5
20	Salesperson Action Report		

Let's put it all together and see how this scenario looks so far.

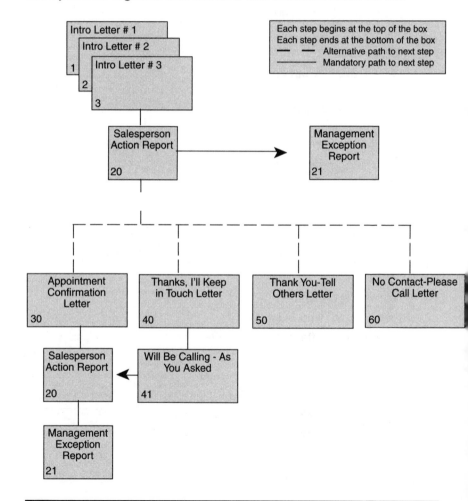

Event	Description	Next Event	Days
1	Introductory Letter #1 -Company	2	5
2	Introductory Letter #2 - Products/Svcs	3	5
3	Introductory Letter #3 - Sales Rep	20	5
20	Sales Rep Action Report	21	5
21	Mgmt Exception Report	21	5
30	Appointment Confirmation Ltr	31	0
31	Salesperson Action Report	21	7
40	Thanks, I'll Keep In Touch	41	Future
41	Will Be Calling - As You Asked	20	5
50	Thank You Letter - Tell Others		
60	No Contact Letter - Please Call	61	5
41	Will Be Calling - As You Asked	42	5

Now you can begin to see how the **Strategic Marketing Plan** works.

What you have seen so far is just a small sample of what can be done. To develop this into a full working scenario, we would have to add several more sequences to handle new contacts—referrals, people we met at a trade show, people who called us, etc. We would also have to add sequences to be used after a meeting, after a demo, after a new sale ... the list goes on and on!

The key is that the Marketing Scenario can be customized so that you can do business the way you want to do business. There is nothing in the system that can't be changed to accommodate your desires.

The important thing to remember is that once a contact is placed on a plan, the system will automatically manage the process and prevent your prospect from ever *falling through the cracks.* The system can automatically process thousands of contacts, all at different points in your scenario, all getting different letters from different salespeople each and every day. When a salesperson begins to slip behind, a management exception report can be generated to let someone know ... ***all according to your plan.***

TACTIC: Direct Voice Mail Marketing Systems

As one known for practicing what I preach, I took inventory not long ago of how I spent my time and calculated the revenue I generate per hour selling. It became painfully obvious that I was spending far too much time talking to the voice mail boxes of potential clients.

I had actually convinced myself that I had no choice, because I felt that nobody could do my job as well as I could and certainly not for hourly wages. Leaving messages in potential client's voice mail boxes was boring, dull and a total waste of my energy, ability, and intellect. I rationalized and kept telling myself that all the best prospects were the hardest to reach, that this was just another "one of those things" I had to do. Perhaps you or your salespeople can relate?

I found a solution… it's called Direct Voice Mail Marketing. The equipment that makes this tactical advantage possible is extremely affordable and can be leased for less than a few dollars a day per salesperson.

First, let me give you an overview of the concept. Then I'll give you the basic information necessary to set up your own calling program utilizing this strategy.

How can prospects with voice mail systems help salespeople sell more?

The invention of voice mail was a blessing or a curse to direct sales professionals, depending upon your perspective.

The Curse … Some viewed this invention as another obstacle that made it even more difficult and time consuming to contact potential customers. Getting past secretaries was hard enough. Now the challenge of getting a decision-maker on the phone had grown tenfold. Upon reaching voice mail, most salespeople hung up in disgust and planned to try again some other day. Salespeople had to work harder and got less desirable results!

The Blessing ... If used correctly, a potential customer's voice mail system can be an invaluable ally. It offers salespeople the opportunity to leave an "uninterrupted commercial" for their product or service with even the most hard to reach decision-maker. Voice mail can make it possible to quickly and easily by-pass "gatekeepers" and communicate what's available to the person who most needs to hear it.

What does Direct Voice Mail Marketing do?

Answer:

It's a technology that makes it possible for salespeople to generate revenue selling, not looking for people to sell to.

Direct Voice Mail Marketing Systems make it possible for less skilled, lower-paid sales support personnel to call prospects and leave pre-recorded voice mail messages using the salesperson's voice. Sales reps can be out selling while prospects who are interested call back to request information or schedule appointments.

There's that old saying, "It's easier to sort prospects than it is to convince them." Salespeople generate more revenue and do it faster when the people they're selling to are interested. Salespeople can spend time selling to decision-makers who have identified and qualified themselves as interested. Closing percentages increase!

Obviously leaving a message in a prospect's voice mail is preferable to hanging up, but by leaving a message, aren't sales reps missing out on the advantages of actually talking to the prospect?

Answer:

In some ways, the opposite is true! Decision-makers are hard to reach and busy. Because of the difficulty in getting through, many salespeople become overzealous and "pushy" when they do make contact. Others call at times that are not convenient for the prospect. Both instances make it easy and in fact actually encourage decision-makers to respond with their knee-jerk "not interested" responses before they even know what they're saying no to.

Well-designed voice mail messages give prospects the ability to listen to what you have to offer them when they have time to listen and can be more receptive. When they are more receptive, they are more likely to listen long enough to find out what is available to them.

Statistically speaking, what advantages does Direct Voice Mail Marketing give a company?

Answer:

An increased number of selling opportunities ...

Sales is and has always been a numbers game. Why should reps make ten or twenty calls to try to get one prospect on the phone to explain what they have to offer when they could have used those same calls to contact many more prospects and convey exactly the same message?

Unlike direct sales or telemarketing, success isn't completely dependent upon initially speaking with the prospect. A salesperson doesn't have to speak with a prospect to find out if he or she is interested in scheduling an appointment or accepting an information pack. What this means for you is that you can more efficiently and cost effectively get the attention of the people to whom you want to sell.

How do using Direct Voice Mail Marketing Systems compare to traditional methods of lead generation like radio, TV, magazine or newspaper advertising?

Answer:

It almost isn't a fair comparison since properly done voice mail marketing messages sound like business calls and aren't thought of as commercials or advertisements.

DVMM VS. Direct Mail ... Voice mail messages get listened to more often than direct mail gets read. Unlike direct mail, that often gets screened, voice mail messages get through to the prospect more often. Ask yourself a simple question: What percentage of the direct mail you receive gets read? By contrast, what percentage of your voice mail messages do you listen to?

DVMM VS. Newspaper or Magazine Print Advertising ... In print advertising terms, your message makes a "front page" impression for the 30-45 seconds the prospect spends listening to your message. Your message gets one hundred percent impact since the prospect is paying attention only to your message during that time.

DVMM VS. Radio and TV Advertising ... Unlike radio or TV, dollars aren't being wasted advertising to people who aren't prospects. Commercials on radio or TV are often unnoticed because people start switching channels.

Additional Flexibility ... Radio commercials, TV advertisements and direct mail advertising pieces can be expensive to create and/or re-create if adjustments need to be made down the road. DVMM messages can be easily adjusted in a matter of minutes and at no expense.

Could potential decision-makers know that they were listening to a recording placed into their voice mail instead of a call made by a real salesperson?

<u>Answer:</u>

Anything is possible, but... pre-recorded marketing messages are the ultimate in quality control! You can be assured that the desired marketing messages are conveyed at the right pitch, pace, enunciation, clarity, and level of enthusiasm each and every time. A machine doesn't fumble, stumble, or stammer. It doesn't get tired or unmotivated. The biggest risk is that your sales representative's messages could sound too good!

As an introduction to the concept of Direct Voice Mail Marketing, let me start by sharing an overview of the basic information necessary to set up your own calling program. There are two approaches. The first approach is characterized by salespeople making their own calls and using the machine to leave "perfect" voice mail messages. The second approach is characterized by organizing an outbound calling team of support personnel who make the calls for the salespeople. Teams can begin with one or two people making calls and can grow into teams of hundreds of callers.

The first approach is very rudimentary and is based on the objective of making every contact with a prospect a perfect one. Salespeople have learned that it is tough to maintain a high energy and enthusiasm level when they end up saying the same old thing over and over again to large groups of prospects with similar or identical needs. Just suppose an insurance salesperson learns of a new product that can help a few hundred current or prospective clients. He can make the calls personally and say the same boring thing, or he can do it once well and let his machine do his talking for him. Those who are interested will call him back. It's much less stressful and tiresome—not to mention less time consuming! In fact, some salespeople who don't have the luxury of clerical support, find they can improve productivity by doing something else while the machine is playing their message into prospect's voice mail boxes. They could be putting together information packets, addressing envelopes, filling out reports, or doing anything else they might need to do.

The second approach goes beyond the goal of getting perfectly worded and delivered messages to the prospects who need to hear them. It seeks to make the approach to identifying interested prospects more efficient and economical. It depends on trained callers who make calls for the salespeople. Salespeople can be out selling while lower paid, support personnel, perform lead generation activities.

To help you put together your own program, we've designed the "Application Analysis" to guide you. The purpose of this analysis is to help you to take into consideration the possible outcomes of call activities and establish reproducible procedures that can be easily taught, easily implemented, and managed consistently. The "Application Analysis" will be helpful regardless of which of the two approaches best suits your objectives. Let me share this guide with you and talk a little about the options and choices it opens up.

Application Analysis:

Target information

Number of times prospects will be called _____ month/year

Approximate interval desired between calls to the same prospects _____
Number of different prospects in a target company _____
Titles of targeted prospects _____
_____
_____

Call list

Organized by recognizable Call Group _____
Are pages numbered within
      each call group _____ or by the overall project _____
Are prospect names listed? Yes _____ Will be determined by caller _____
Alphabetical order by company name _____
Age of list? _____ Accuracy of phone numbers? (1-10) _____

Sales representative information

Use marketing rep approach ___ Use sales representative approach ___
Number of different sales representatives _____
      # of different messages per rep _____

Script checklist: (Note any exceptions)

ID prospect and ask for voice mail _____
Voice mail message(s) _____
If prospect answers the phone _____
Other _____ _____

Contingencies:

How long should caller wait on hold? _____
If prospect picks up the phone? _____

If there is no voice mail at that company? _____

If prospect is at another location? _____

Local _____

Long Distance _____

If the prospect has been replaced/vacant position? _____

Your plans/ system of notifying us of call-ins when multiple wave marketing is in place: _____

_____

_____

_____

How you wish to be notified of actual conversations that generate interest

_____

_____

How and how often you wish to have completed reports returned to you _

_____

Target Information

Have you established who you want called? Have you developed a plan for how many times each prospect will be contacted and the intervals between those contacts? At first, I suggest that you use your best judgement and that you keep things simple.

In the long run, I would encourage you to try different call frequencies and call intervals. Measure and record the results until you find out what works the best for your company. Just suppose "Company A" has one product to sell and has unlimited prospects, a plan to deliver one voice mail message per year, per prospect, might be enough. By comparison, if "Company B" has multiple products and services and has a finite territory, a better strategy would be to call prospects once a month with different scripts, promoting different products or services with each call.

If you don't get the response you desire, there are only two possible reasons.

1) You're calling on the wrong person.

2) Your message is ineffective. If your message is ineffective, there could be two reasons.

> A) The content lacks impact (dull, boring, too long, etc.)

> B) The timing of your call wasn't appropriate.

For example, a message left for a sales manager that promotes pre-employment testing may fail to generate interest if he or she isn't hiring.

Do calls need to be made to multiple people within prospective client companies? Can the same messages be used or must different messages be developed to address different concerns?

If you want to set up a lead generating, outbound call center utilizing Direct Voice Mail Marketing Systems, you would be wise to invest considerable time and energy deciding on your message and the strategy for delivering that message.

Ask yourself four questions when it comes time to determine your message:

1) Who are your prospects?

2) What problems do they have that your product or service can address?

3) What product(s)/service(s) do you have to address their problems?

4) What are the benefits they will receive by using your product(s)/service(s)?

Following this method, developing a strategy to communicate what to offer is very simple. Just design benefit-oriented scripts that, over a period of time, let your prospects know who you are and what your company can do.

Those who are interested will call back and the sales process will be underway.

When callers are being used to support your sales team, it is also important to let them know the various titles that a potential decision-maker could use. For example, don't assume that your callers will automatically know that if a company doesn't have a vice president of sales, they might still have a person with those responsibilities going by the title of sales executive or sales manager.

Call List

An effective and efficient lead generation effort begins with a well-developed and organized call list. Ideally, call groups should be established and the pages on the list should be numbered. For example, just suppose there are 1000 prospects in the state of New Jersey for your product. Experience suggests that you should have those prospects organized geographically and/or alphabetically by company name. You might want to have five or ten call groups of 100 or 200 prospects.

I suggest that you create lists alphabetically by company name, not by prospect name. Two reasons have motivated my choice. When interested prospects call in, sometimes it's hard to understand their names and guess at the spellings. Secondly, prospects change companies and get promoted more often than companies change names. Using company names will make your prospects easier to track.

If it is difficult to get a list with accurate names, there is a simple solution. As a matter of fact, rarely do I give my callers lists with prospect's names. They are instructed to call with a simple script like this:

"Hi, I was wanting to send some information to your vice president of sales. To whom do I need to address it? Could you help me spell that? Could you transfer me into his/her voice mail?"

It's fast, easy, accurate, and effective. Callers don't waste time correcting lists where changes have taken place.

Sales Representative Information

How should the call be positioned? Should the call recipient believe that the sales representative made the call? Or should the call recipient believe he was contacted by a marketing representative? A "marketing rep approach" might tend to make a small company seem larger, while the other approach might be perceived as more personal. Depending on how you want to be perceived, one route or the other might be best for your company.

Script Checklist

A solid plan for DVMM will need to be supported by carefully worded messages. Those messages should be the epitome of short, sweet, and to the point. Messages longer than thirty or forty seconds are risky. In any case, at a bare minimum, scripts should be developed for the following situations:

- To identify the prospect and ask for voice mail

- To peak curiosity and generate a return call

- To peak curiosity and generate interest in receiving a follow up phone call or information packet when a prospect actually picks up the phone

- To handle the "What kind of information do you want to send?" and "What does your company do?" questions asked by prospects and the personal assistants who answer their lines.

Contingencies

Callers will need special instructions. You should decide several things and establish the rules so there is as little guesswork as possible.

1) Hold

Depending on the size and importance of the companies and prospects being called, hold times may vary. If there are ten thousand other prospects to be talking to, a caller waiting on hold for five minutes could be a terrible waste of time and resources. When the number of potential prospects is unlimited, a five-minute wait costs your company the opportunity to have contacted several other companies in that same period of time. On the other hand, if your prospect list is limited and closer to finite, a minute or two may not be unreasonable.

2) What if the prospect picks up the phone or there is no voice mail?

If the callers are properly trained and the scripts are good ones, situations like this will be the exception, rather than the rule. What the caller should do at this point is a matter of personal preference.

If you don't want anybody but your salespeople talking to the prospect, you may instruct the caller to hang up. If nine out of ten calls end up reaching voice mail, you may not care if your salespeople have to make ten percent of the calls again. At least they are out selling while the other ninety percent of the calls were being made!

On the other hand, why duplicate ten percent of your calling effort when with a little training and a few basic scripts, the caller could easily determine possible interest and promise follow-up from a salesperson.

3) What if the prospect is at another location?

Situations sometimes occur where the person the caller wants to leave a message for is located somewhere else. If the other location is across town and in the same calling territory, you may want to instruct the caller to write down the number, note the variance on the call sheet, and proceed to call them. If the other location is in another territory or likely to appear on another call list, you may want the caller to make a note on the call sheet and not call the new location. It could be embarrassing for your company to leave the same message more than once for the same person.

4) Caller and salesperson communication

There needs to be a simple procedure for salespeople to notify callers when interested prospects call in to request information packets or schedule appointments.

On the flip-side, it's also important to have a way to let salespeople know when to follow–up with prospects who indicated interest during actual conversations with callers.

This is particularly important when part of your company's marketing strategy includes multiple calls or "wave marketing". This is where being able to refer to specific pages within call groups on call lists is an obvious necessity.

5) Call Codes

If you set-up a relatively large or complex calling program it will help you to set up a system of codes that indicate things like:

• When the last voice mail message was left

• The date each call was completed

• What happened on each call.

Here is a list of the codes used as part of our calling program. You may develop your own or use these.

Call Activity Codes

TLH-Too Long on Hold
PMI-Personal Message, Interested
PMN-Personal Message, Not interested
SI-Send Information

SCR-Screened by the receptionist
NVM-No Voice Mail
MBF- Mail Box was Full (When you get to someone who has voice mail, but it's full)
NHQ-Not Head-Quarters (When they say you need to call some other location)
WG-Wouldn't Give (When the receptionist refuses to give you the name)
CBL-Call Back Later (When you speak to the person and they are too busy to speak)
RMC-Returned My Call (They have shown enough interest to call us back)

Combination Codes

RMC/NI-They returned our call, but weren't interested. Don't call them again
RMC/SI- They returned our call and were interested. We sent them information. Don't call them again.
PMI/SI- We spoke with them and they were interested. We sent them information. Don't call them again.

Call Number Codes

After the call has been successfully completed

First Call- Place a 1 to the left of their name

Second Call- Circle the 1 that is next to their name

Third Call- Place an X over the Circle with the 1 inside of it.

By now you should have a conceptual understanding of this marketing strategy. You should also have a good feeling about how to actually implement a calling program of your own. It's not very difficult. Feel free to give us a call if you have questions. We will be glad to help.

TACTIC: Audio Business Cards/CD-Rom Presentations

I had a problem. My company launched a telesales campaign to sell skill, attitude and personality assessment tools over the telephone. It's always a two-part sale. The first part is a conceptual sale on the value of utilizing assessment tools. The second part is a matter of finding out specific customer needs and prescribing assessment packages that will address those needs.

The first part of the sales effort is boring and repetitive for the salesperson, but it's absolutely necessary to create the start of a long-term business relationship. It's also hard to maintain interest long enough to get to part two of the sales effort if it's not done well.

I was visiting with a client of mine whose father in law, Stewart Meyers, happened to be a top producing life insurance agent in Oklahoma City. He approximately doubled his business by developing an "audio cassette interview." He found it highly effective at separating those prospects who were interested from those who weren't without unnecessarily wasting his time. It gave him the ability to be making multiple presentations, simultaneously, nationwide!

I've found through personal experience that by applying this tactic our telephone bills diminished, salespeople spent less time engaged in low probability sales opportunities, and they generated more sales. As an added bonus, prospects seemed to appreciate having the flexibility of listening to our information at their convenience. Several commented that they liked the approach because it wasn't pushy.

I particularly liked knowing that the message and the quality of its delivery was consistent and manageable. The training time necessary to get a new salesperson up to speed was reduced by fifty percent since they really only had to focus on the second; and by far, the most important part of the presentation process.

If your budget is larger and you prefer a multi-media approach, it's possible to have an entire audio-visual presentation put onto a CD-ROM.

TACTIC: Web Page/Fax Pack/ Fax On Demand

I want to touch on these topics in the context of improving your consideration rate, reducing sales time, and the cost of sales.

Maybe you don't buy things from the internet. Maybe you don't do research on the internet for products or services you're interested in. Millions of other people do. People can't buy what they don't know about from people they don't know exist.

I had a client who loved to preach that "Time kills all deals!" If you make contact with a potential client who wants information, you need to give it to them as fast as possible. If you don't have a budget that allows for "Overnight Priority Mail" for every information packet request, consider having a "Fax Packet" that an administrative support person can send out immediately. If you have a web page, you can suggest that they check it out in the meantime. These options can also minimize your printing budget.

Some companies have toll free numbers with a menu of choices whereby prospects can have up to the minute information faxed to them electronically without tying up your staff or budget getting it to them. It's called "Fax on Demand" and is easy and relatively inexpensive to set up.

For example, let's say a wholesale food distributor has clients calling sales or customer service people for inventory and pricing information. Why allow productive selling to take a back seat to errands that can be handled faster, more conveniently, and more cost effectively? (Don't worry about competitors getting your prices. They already have them.) The customer service lines could all be busy; the salesperson may be on an appointment. Delays frustrate customers. Even if a customer service representative or a salesperson knew the answers off the top of his head; when customers can't reach someone who knows, they get frustrated. Information like this could just as easily be posted on a web-site.

By no means am I saying that you have to take these approaches when filling requests for information, but it's nice to have options, particularly when they reduce hard costs and time spent on non-selling activities.

TACTIC: Simplified Order Processing

Several years ago I did some work with the Army National Guard to improve their recruiting. There were a lot of areas in their sales process that needed fixing. There were good recruiters being paid the same as bad recruiters who hadn't signed up a single recruit in six months and, believe me, issues like this were the tip of the iceberg.

Almost every strategy and tactic in this book if applied to it's fullest, wouldn't have made much of a difference until one key issue was resolved. That issue was the completion of new recruit enlistment packets. They took a full day; usually longer, to fill out and that's if everything went smoothly and there weren't special requests or waivers that needed special attention. A finished packet looked like a volume of a small encyclopedia. Everything had to be in order and it had to be right. If it wasn't, reprimands and unfavorable job evaluations were sure to follow.

Reality became clear. The more enlistments a recruiter achieved, the more (boring, repetitive & tedious) work he created for himself. On average, the recruiters did just well enough to keep from getting fired. Some didn't even do that well. If you saw the packets, you probably wouldn't blame them.

I noticed that there was clerical staff, clearly capable of this type of work, with idle time. It seemed like common sense to ask why they didn't help? "Leadership" adamantly informed me that filling out packets was the recruiter's job. "Why," I asked? The response was, "Because, that's the way we do it and we will continue to do it that way."

Nothing frustrates salespeople more than unnecessary paperwork. Are your salespeople getting punished for making a sale? Are they held hostage by antiquated systems for no good reason other than resistance to change? With the technology available, there is no reason for double and triple entry of data! If your process is unnecessarily long, fix it.

Section 7: Conclusion

We have learned a tremendous amount of valuable information from our clients and prospective clients. We hope that what we have chosen to share is the best of what we have learned. There is no need for you, anyone in your company, or anyone else you care about to suffer financial losses and/or waste years of hard work learning these lessons through trial and error.

There is one last observation we feel compelled to share. One of the most frequent mistakes is the failure by key executives to take action and make necessary improvements. These ideas and strategies are worthless unless you or the people you hire have the guts to implement them.

We can't count the number times we have heard executives exhibit what they feel are masterful rationalizations about why they "can't" or "shouldn't" fix what they know is broken. They live in denial hoping problems will go unnoticed or evaporate. Some figure they would be better off not calling attention to a problem that, until now, they didn't even know about.

As a child, I was told that the ostriches would bury their heads in the sand as form of protection or escape from perceived danger. As an adult, I'm amazed that highly paid executives too often imitate behavioral patterns that a typical first grader recognizes as absurd! There are too many executives and managers whose effort is the equivalent of re-arranging deck chairs on the Titanic! They look busy and the bustle of activity makes people feel good, but can't keep the ship from sinking.

Additionally, people die from terminal illnesses every day. Many of those deaths are premature, if not totally unnecessary because of one simple problem. The afflicted simply ignored the symptoms and pain until they couldn't tolerate it any longer. When they finally decided to do something about it, it was too late.

We want to encourage you to somehow find it within yourself to do what you know must be done. There will be others who will resist your proposed changes; sometimes adamantly. Drive on and finish your mission anyway! Just get it done!

You have been served a smorgasboard of ideas and strategies that can help you make a positive difference in your organization. We have attempted to give you all the information you need to make the changes you feel you must. If you liked what you read, but don't feel you have the time, expertise or energy to implement it, call us. We will be glad to discuss your challenges and would be pleased to help.

How to Contact the Authors:

Mason Duchatschek, Allen Minster
AMO-Employer Services, Inc.
P.O. Box 159
Fenton, MO 63026
Masonduke@aol.com
www.amo-es.com
800-245-0445

Call Us To Order Additional Copies:

It's a great gift idea!

Quantity discounts are available! Call for pricing!

Want more great ideas?
Subscriptions to our electronic newsletter are FREE!

Visit our web site at **www.amo-es.com** to subscribe to our **electronic newsletter**. Registering is free, but the information contained in the newsletter could be worth a fortune !

Need an expert speaker for your ...

Convention,
Trade Show,
Association Meeting, or
Sales Conference ?

Custom programs and seminars are available in formats ranging from a 30-minute keynote to a full day workshop ! Call for available dates !

The authors have been featured in national publications like Selling magazine, Selling Power magazine, Office World News, and numerous other trade journals, business journals, and newspapers. **Don't miss them live !**

SUCCESS STORIES WANTED !

So that others can benefit and learn from your experiences, please send us your stories ! Let us know how the information and ideas in this book have helped you and your organization improve. If we use your story in any future editions, books, or programs, we will be happy to provide you with a complimentary, autographed copy of our latest book.

Mail stories to:
Performance Press Worldwide, Inc.
Attn: Success Stories
28 Starboard Drive
Crystal City, MO 63019

DO YOU REALIZE HOW GOOD YOUR SALES TEAM COULD BE?

WANT TO FIND OUT . . . FOR FREE?

The Sales Potential Evaluation Program: We have a computer program that can help you better understand the relationship between your current sales process and the revenue it generates. We will be happy to perform a free computerized analysis for you. Call us today!

If you don't have the time or expertise to make the necessary changes yourself, call and ask about our consulting services!

Employee Selection Systems

Employee Development Systems

Direct Voice Mail Marketing Systems

Sales Process Analysis/Re-engineering

Sales Force Automation Systems

On-line Recruiting Services